Forts for Kids

Designs & Illustrations
by

David Stiles

W9-BOB-351

LYONS PRESS
Guilford, Connecticut

An imprint of Globe Pequot Press

Lyons Press is an imprint of Globe Pequot Press.

Designed and illustrated by David Stiles

Edited by Toby Haynes

Library of Congress Cataloging-in-Publication Data is available on file.

ISBN 978-0-7627-6453-2

Printed in the United States of America

10 9 8 7 6 5 4 3 2 1

Disclaimer: David and Jeanie Stiles make no express or implied warranties, including warranties of performance, merchantability, and fitness for a particular purpose, regarding this information. Your use of this information is at your own risk. You assume full responsibility and risk of loss resulting from the use of this information. The authors and publisher will not be responsible for any direct, special, indirect, incidental, consequential, or punitive damages or other damages whatsoever.

Since many of our readers invariably change our plans to fit their particular needs, we assume that they will seek qualified, licensed architects or engineers to make more detailed plans for submission to their local building and health departments, as required.

Note: Every effort has been made to design all the projects in this book to be safe and easy to build; however, it is impossible to predict every situation and the ability of each carpenter who builds our projects. Therefore, it is advised that the reader seek advice from a competent, on-site professional builder.

TABLE OF CONTENTS

Acknowledgments

There are three people I would like to mention. The first is Tom Kenly, the director at my summer camp in New Hampshire, where each summer the campers built a cabin, made their own bows and arrows, and split the firewood for the camp stove. He provided a section in the woods called "Monkey Town," where campers built their own treehouses, some connected to each other by ladders. Monkey Town even had its own elected mayor, Monkey Town money, and exciting carnivals.

The second person I never actually met. He is Dan Beard, who started the Boy Scouts of America back in the early 1900s. His drawings in the *Boy Scout Handbook* fascinated me and were my inspiration for years to come. Like myself, Dan Beard lived in New York City, was a member of the Society of Illustrators, and spent a lot of time outdoors.

Last, but definitely not least, is my father, who spent his life as a career officer in the U.S. Navy. His secret passion was drawing. As a young boy watching him make a quick sketch of a PT boat, I got the idea that perhaps I too could someday draw. Without his early guidance this book would not have been written.

A brief
History of Forts

MEDIEVAL FORT

Fortified City
Carcassonne
France

The much imitated style of the Norman castle was introduced in 1066 with the Norman invasion of Britain. Their use of stone as a building material replaced the Anglo-Saxon wood stockade.

STOCKADE FORT

In the United States, forts were built along trails to protect travelers, provide a place of refuge in case of an Indian attack, and establish trading posts. Frontiersmen built forts out of the abundant timber in the region. Often these forts bloomed into thriving communities as more and more settlers traveled across the country.

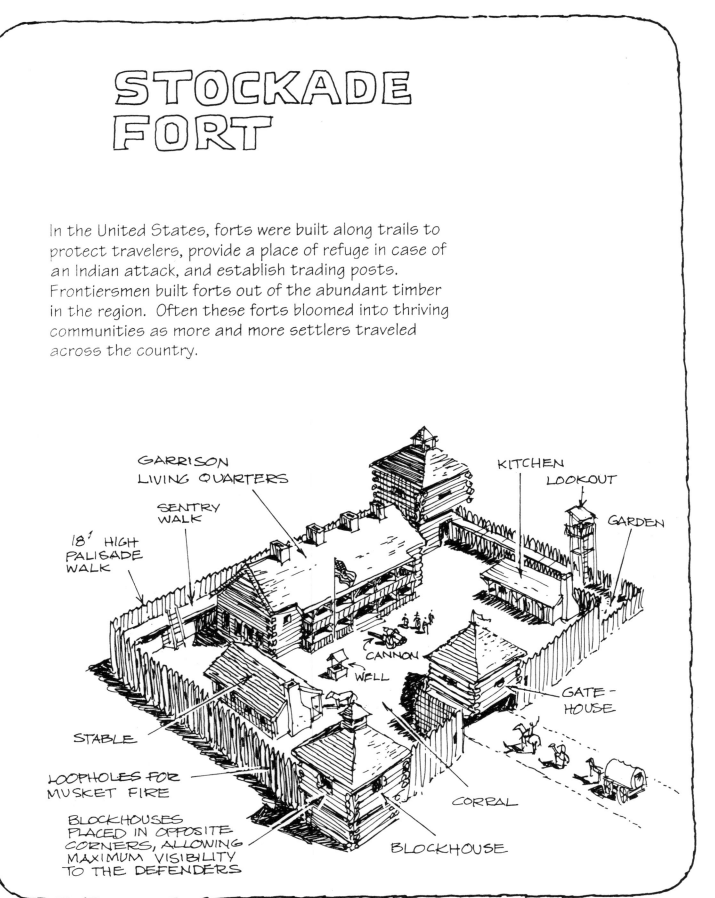

GARRISON LIVING QUARTERS

SENTRY WALK

18' HIGH PALISADE WALK

KITCHEN

LOOKOUT

GARDEN

CANNON

WELL

GATE-HOUSE

STABLE

LOOPHOLES FOR MUSKET FIRE

BLOCKHOUSES PLACED IN OPPOSITE CORNERS, ALLOWING MAXIMUM VISIBILITY TO THE DEFENDERS

CORRAL

BLOCKHOUSE

FORTS OF THE FUTURE

Forts of the future are open to your own imagination. They may be shiny skyscrapers with stainless-steel bastions and computerized laser gun turrets.

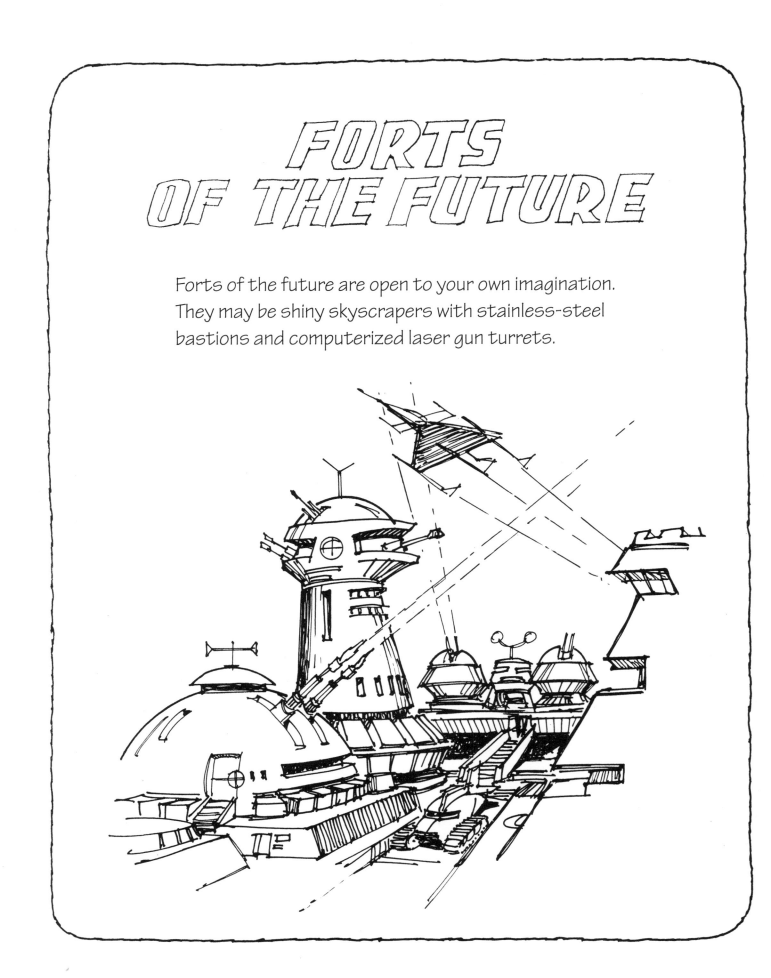

Building Tips

ABBREVIATIONS

DIA. = Diameter
&   = And
EXT. = Exterior
INT. = Interior
Galv. = Galvanized
O.C. = On Center
PLY. = Plywood
T&G = Tongue and Groove
P.T.   = Pressure-Treated Wood

Planning a Fort

When I was a small boy I decided to build a clubhouse out of lumber that I bought with my allowance. I ordered all the lumber and began to hammer the pieces together without giving it much thought. Once I got the frame up, I began to realize that I had not taken into account how the wallboards would be attached, how the corners would join, and how the various pieces would overlap. It was then that I realized how important it was to make plans before starting a project. I vowed to myself that I would never make that mistake again.

Take a box, for example. You might think that making a box would be very simple, but actually there are many things to consider.

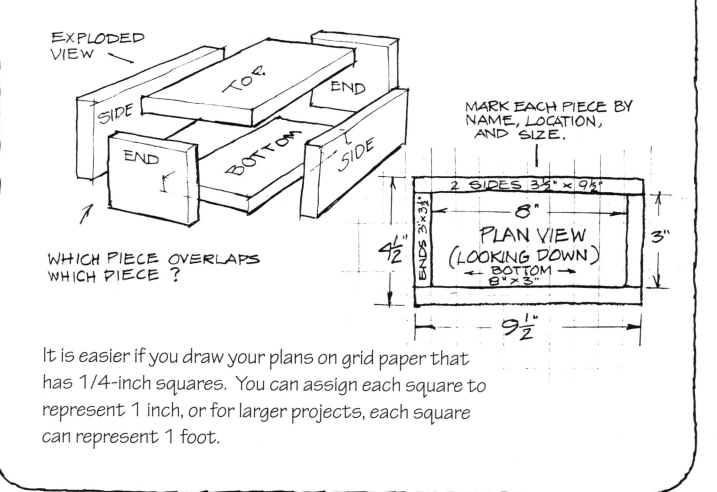

EXPLODED VIEW

SIDE
TOP
END
END
BOTTOM
SIDE

WHICH PIECE OVERLAPS WHICH PIECE?

MARK EACH PIECE BY NAME, LOCATION, AND SIZE.

2 SIDES 3½" × 9½"

ENDS 3" × 3½"

8"

PLAN VIEW
(LOOKING DOWN)
← BOTTOM →
8" × 3"

4½"

3"

9½"

It is easier if you draw your plans on grid paper that has 1/4-inch squares. You can assign each square to represent 1 inch, or for larger projects, each square can represent 1 foot.

Finding Wood

Before you spend your allowance on wood for the fort, look around the neighborhood and see if there isn't any lumber free for the taking. Many new houses being built have waste bins filled with quantities of useful lumber and plywood. Be sure to ask the builder before taking any.

Often, old decks are replaced with new lumber and the perfectly usable old lumber is carted away to the town dump. Ask permission at the dump to take some of the pieces home.

Tree logs can be saved from being chopped up in a chipper. Ask the tree specialists in your neighborhood to save them for you.

Buying Lumber

1. Check your local home improvement stores where the prices are cheaper and the lumber is kept dry because it is stored inside. They will generally cut it up for you as long as you give them a cutting plan.

2. Use only pressure-treated wood marked "for ground contact" for posts that will be buried in the ground.

3. Choose each piece carefully and sight down along the edge to make sure it is straight and has few defects.

4. Clear lumber (wood that has no knots) is three times more expensive than #2 construction-grade lumber. You can save money by buying extra-long #2-grade boards and cutting out just the good portions.

5. If you are ordering lumber to be delivered from the lumberyard, order 10% more lumber than you need and send back the unusable pieces. Expect to pay a 15% restocking fee, but it is worth it.

6. If you are using recycled lumber, you might have to redesign your plans to match the available materials.

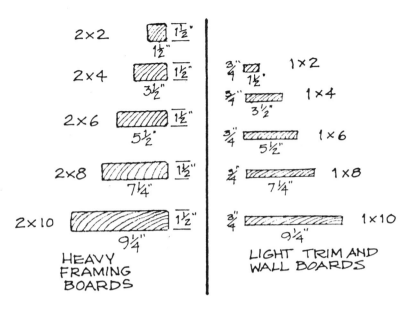

2×2 1½" 1½"
2×4 1½" 3½"
2×6 1½" 5½"
2×8 1½" 7¼"
2×10 1½" 9¼"

HEAVY FRAMING BOARDS

¾" 1½" 1×2
¾" 3½" 1×4
¾" 5½" 1×6
¾" 7¼" 1×8
¾" 9¼" 1×10

LIGHT TRIM AND WALL BOARDS

Lumber Sizes

Lumber sizes are not what they seem, because the lumber is dressed (planed and sanded) to a smaller size before it leaves the mill. For instance, a 2x4 actually measures 1 1/2" x 3 1/2" (or 1/2" less on two sides). Tip: Pressure-treated lumber may vary slightly in dimension.

When choosing lumber for your fort, keep in mind how the grain of the lumber is positioned to support the load it is intended for. Used flat, as in deck boards, it is weakest. When used on edge, as for floor joists, it is stronger, and when used vertically, as in posts, it is strongest. (See illustration below.)

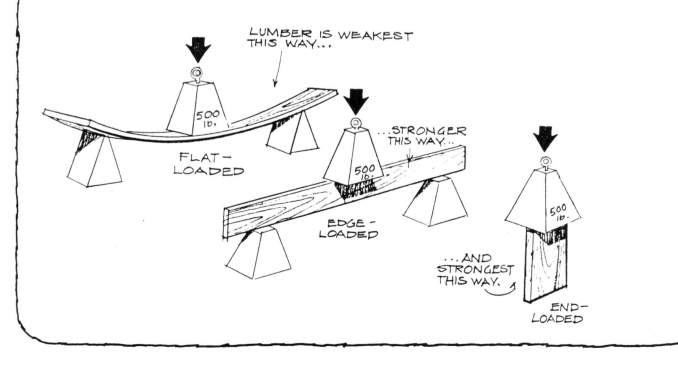

LUMBER IS WEAKEST THIS WAY...

FLAT-LOADED

...STRONGER THIS WAY...

EDGE-LOADED

...AND STRONGEST THIS WAY.

END-LOADED

Where to Build Your Fort

Will your neighbors complain? If you think they might, go over to them, show them a picture of what you're planning to build on your property, and ask their advice. Getting them involved means they are less likely to complain. To give an idea of how the fort will look, you can take a photo of the proposed location, print it, and draw the fort onto the picture.

Is the Fort Accessible?

If the fort is going to be built in the woods, it may be difficult to carry your materials to the site. You also might need to be closer to the house to run an extension cord for any electric tools.

Is the Fort Legal?

Most communities don't require building permits for temporary play structures such as forts, playhouses, and treehouses less than 200 square feet in area—but you should check with your local officials just to be sure.

NAILS

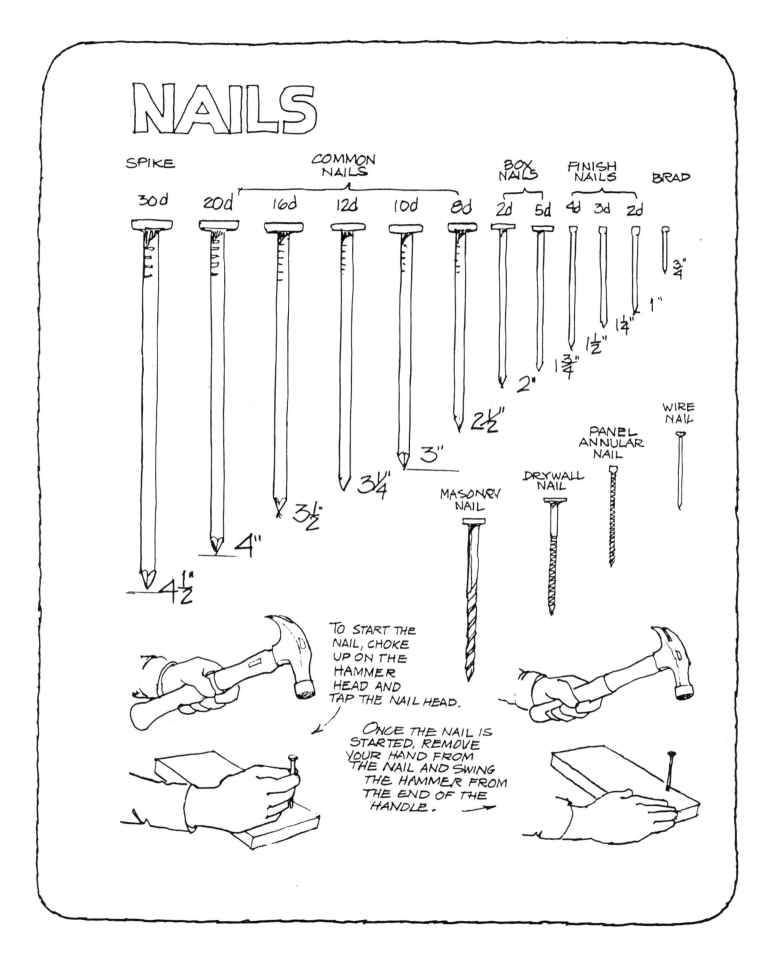

SPIKE

COMMON NAILS

BOX NAILS

FINISH NAILS

BRAD

30d 20d 16d 12d 10d 8d 2d 5d 4d 3d 2d

3/4"

1"

1¼"

1½"

1¾"

2"

2½"

3"

3¼"

3½"

4"

4½"

MASONRY NAIL

DRYWALL NAIL

PANEL ANNULAR NAIL

WIRE NAIL

TO START THE NAIL, CHOKE UP ON THE HAMMER HEAD AND TAP THE NAIL HEAD.

ONCE THE NAIL IS STARTED, REMOVE YOUR HAND FROM THE NAIL AND SWING THE HAMMER FROM THE END OF THE HANDLE.

Nailing

Dad - All you have to do is drill some holes in the beams and let the kids do the rest. The hole size should match the diameter of the nails so that the kids will be able to push the nails into the holes and hammer them into the posts.

Make sure the beams are LEVEL before nailing.

4X4 POST

10d or # 16d GALVANIZED COMMON NAILS

20 oz.

BEAM

The predrilled hole holds the nail in place and makes it easier for kids to hammer the nail in without bending it.

LEVEL HELD BY TAPE

TAPE

If you think that you may need to remove the nails later, use double-headed (duplex) nails, which can be easily removed using a wrecking bar.

WRECKING BAR

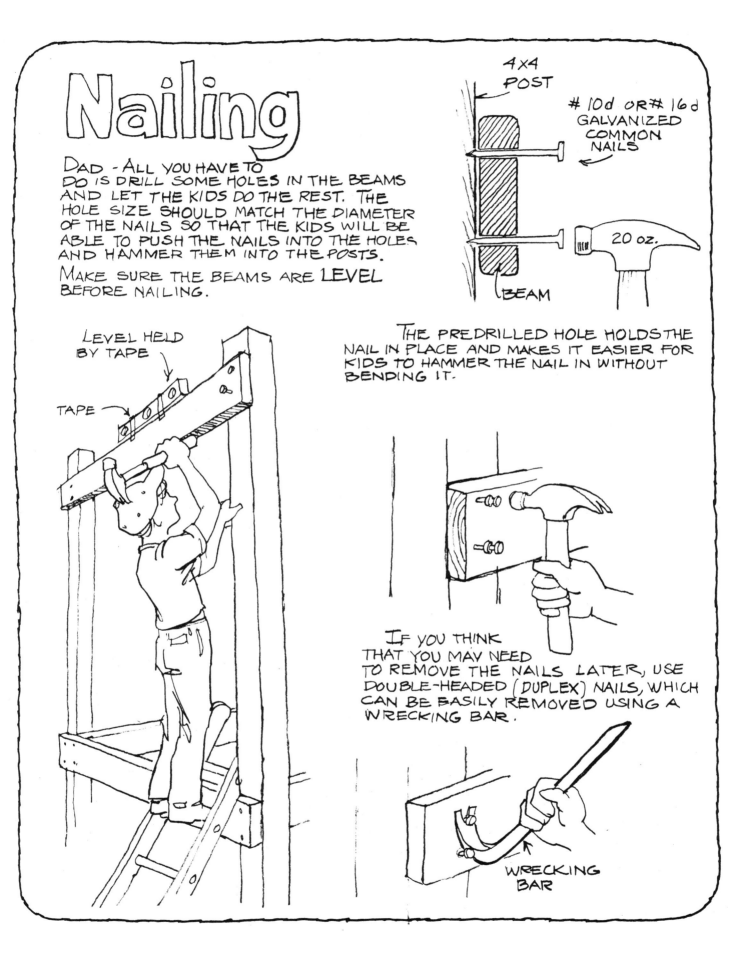

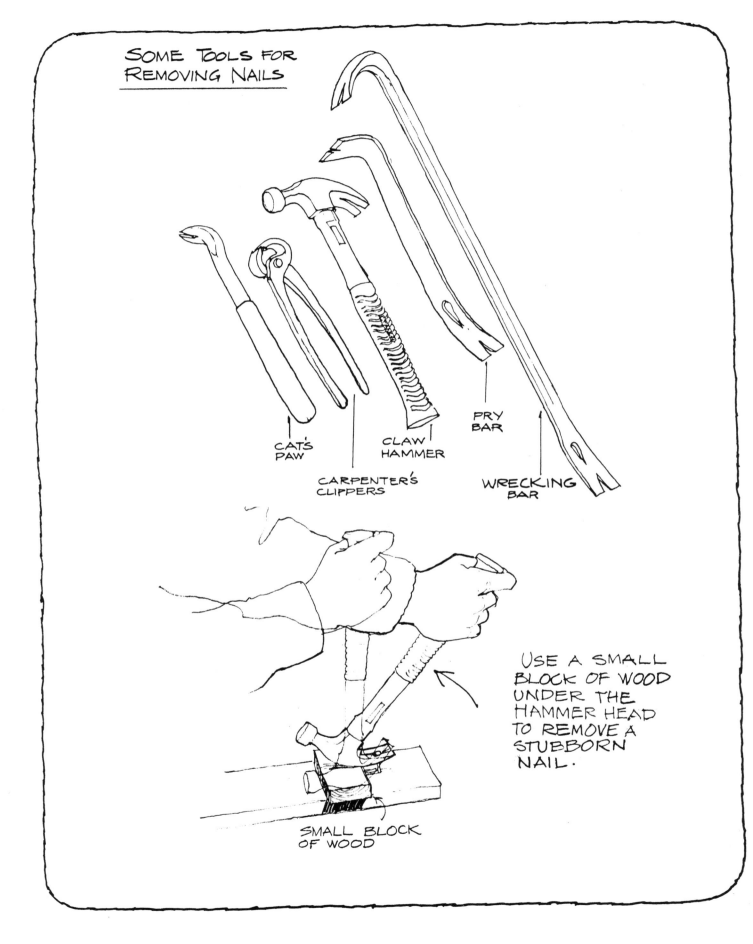

SOME TOOLS FOR REMOVING NAILS

CAT'S PAW

CARPENTER'S CLIPPERS

CLAW HAMMER

PRY BAR

WRECKING BAR

USE A SMALL BLOCK OF WOOD UNDER THE HAMMER HEAD TO REMOVE A STUBBORN NAIL.

SMALL BLOCK OF WOOD

SCREWS

TYPICAL SCREW SIZES & LENGTHS

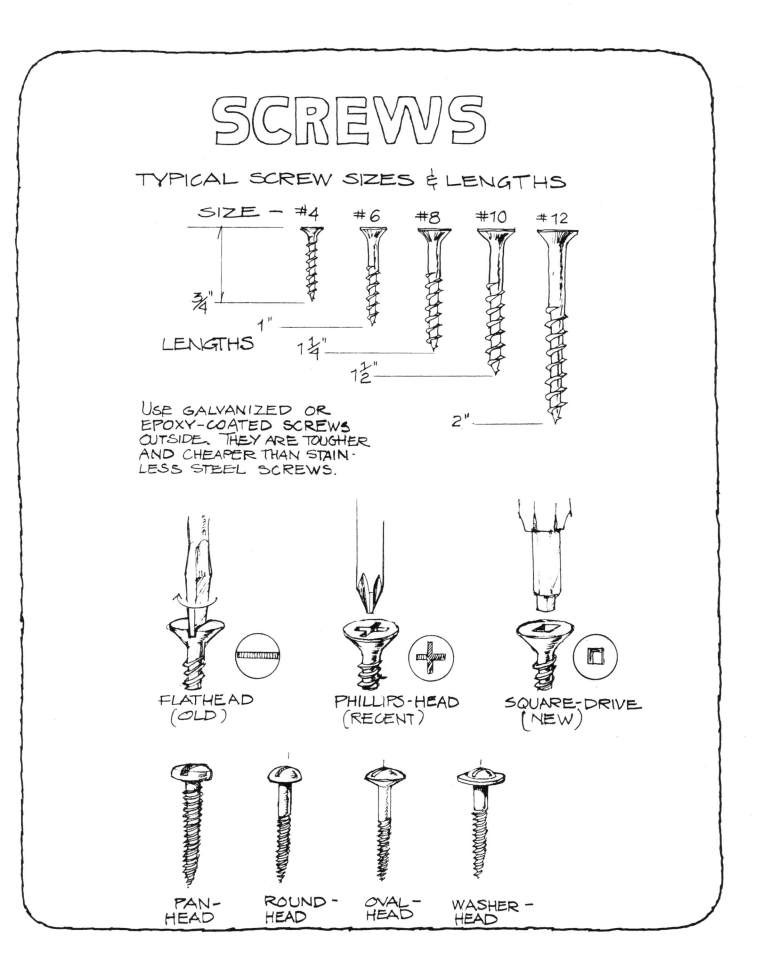

SIZE — #4   #6   #8   #10   #12

3/4"

LENGTHS   1"

1 1/4"

1 1/2"

Use galvanized or epoxy-coated screws outside. They are tougher and cheaper than stainless steel screws.

2"

FLATHEAD (OLD)

PHILLIPS-HEAD (RECENT)

SQUARE-DRIVE (NEW)

PAN-HEAD   ROUND-HEAD   OVAL-HEAD   WASHER-HEAD

Sawing

Dad: Sawing can be difficult for a young child, because he or she may find it hard to keep the saw straight and the board from shifting at the same time. To make this easier, you can build this simple two-piece jig to hold the boards. Make an allowance for a slot between the two 2x4s just wide enough for the saw blade to pass through easily. Clamp the jig and the board to a sawhorse. The sawhorse should be approximately the height of the child's waist.

Note: If you are working with pressure-treated wood, be sure to wear work gloves and do not breathe sawdust.

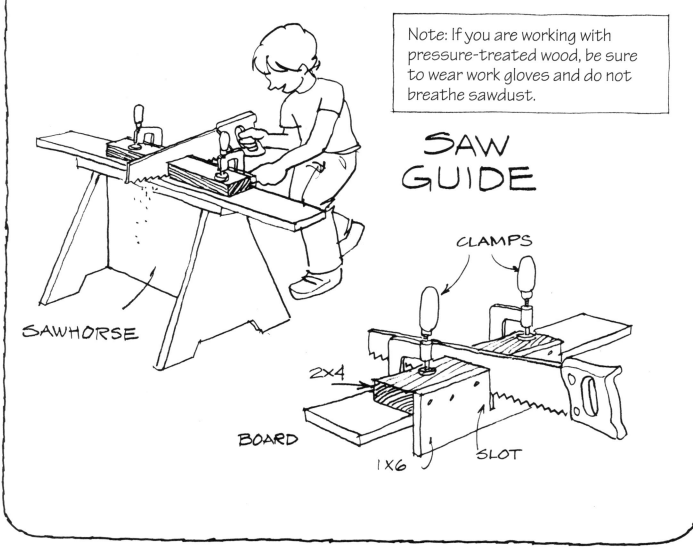

SAWHORSE

SAW GUIDE

CLAMPS

2x4

BOARD

1X6

SLOT

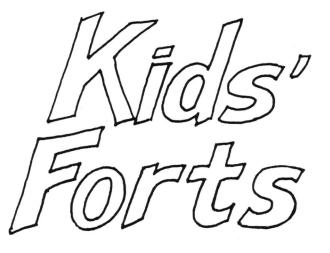

Kids' Forts

A fort is a very special place where you can relax and feel safe. It is a place to be by yourself in your own little world, or to share with a very good friend. It is a place that is just your size—made just for you.

Once you are comfortable in your fort, your imagination can change it into anything from a giant's dungeon, to a secret cave beneath the earth, to a spaceship taking you on a fantastic voyage through the stars.

Kids: Consult your parents before building any of these forts, and before using any tools that you are unfamiliar with.

SECRET HIDEAWAYS

It's easy to make a secret hideaway into a fort or just a good place to read. Sometimes all you need is a blanket or pillows.

TAKE A FLASH-LIGHT WITH YOU UNDER THE BLANKET TO HELP YOU SEE.

BATH TOWELS TO COVER CRACKS

BLANKETS

TABLE

PILLOWS

RUG

SOFA PILLOWS STACKED AGAINST EACH OTHER

PILLOWS

BLANKET

CHAIRS

2 CHAIRS

REFRIGERATOR BOX FORT

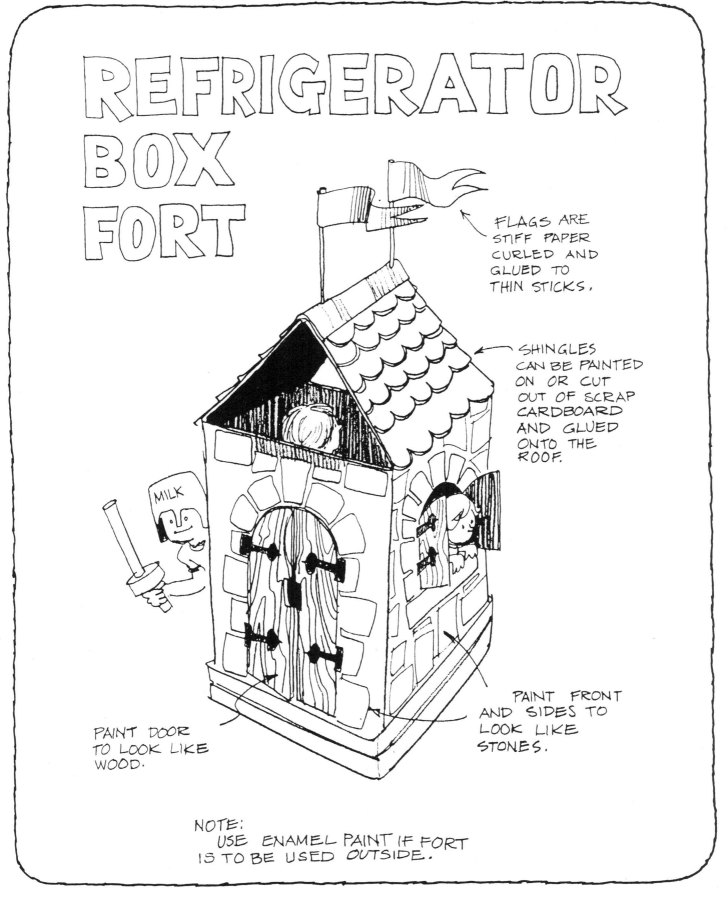

FLAGS ARE STIFF PAPER CURLED AND GLUED TO THIN STICKS.

SHINGLES CAN BE PAINTED ON OR CUT OUT OF SCRAP CARDBOARD AND GLUED ONTO THE ROOF.

MILK

PAINT FRONT AND SIDES TO LOOK LIKE STONES.

PAINT DOOR TO LOOK LIKE WOOD.

NOTE:
USE ENAMEL PAINT IF FORT IS TO BE USED OUTSIDE.

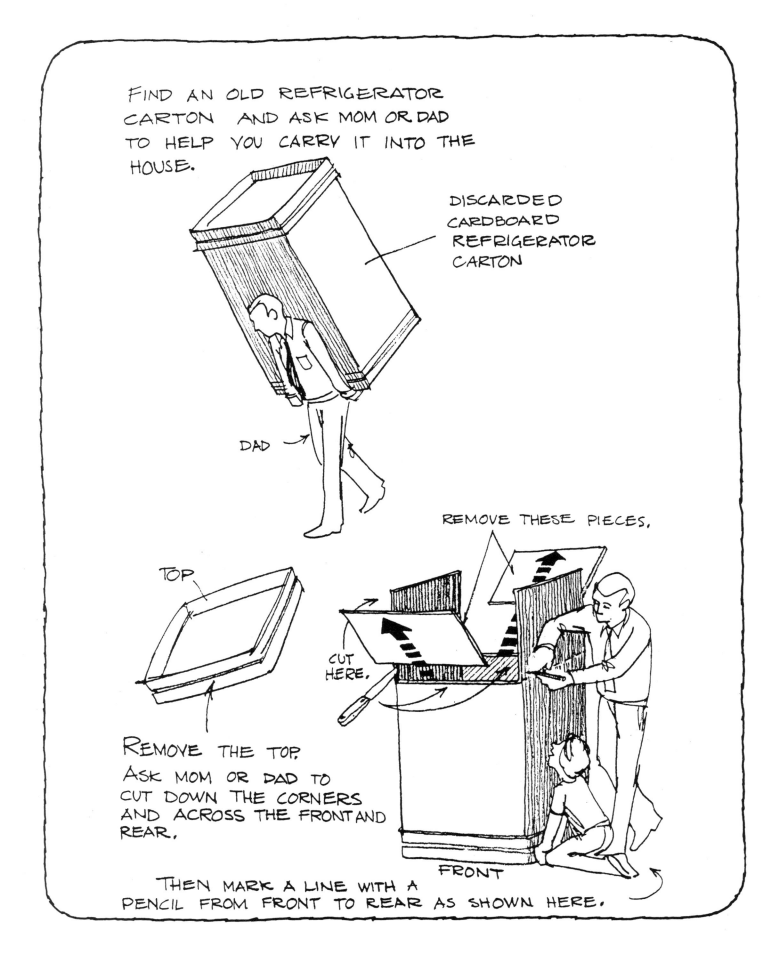

FIND AN OLD REFRIGERATOR CARTON AND ASK MOM OR DAD TO HELP YOU CARRY IT INTO THE HOUSE.

DISCARDED CARDBOARD REFRIGERATOR CARTON

DAD

REMOVE THESE PIECES.

TOP

CUT HERE.

REMOVE THE TOP. ASK MOM OR DAD TO CUT DOWN THE CORNERS AND ACROSS THE FRONT AND REAR.

FRONT

THEN MARK A LINE WITH A PENCIL FROM FRONT TO REAR AS SHOWN HERE.

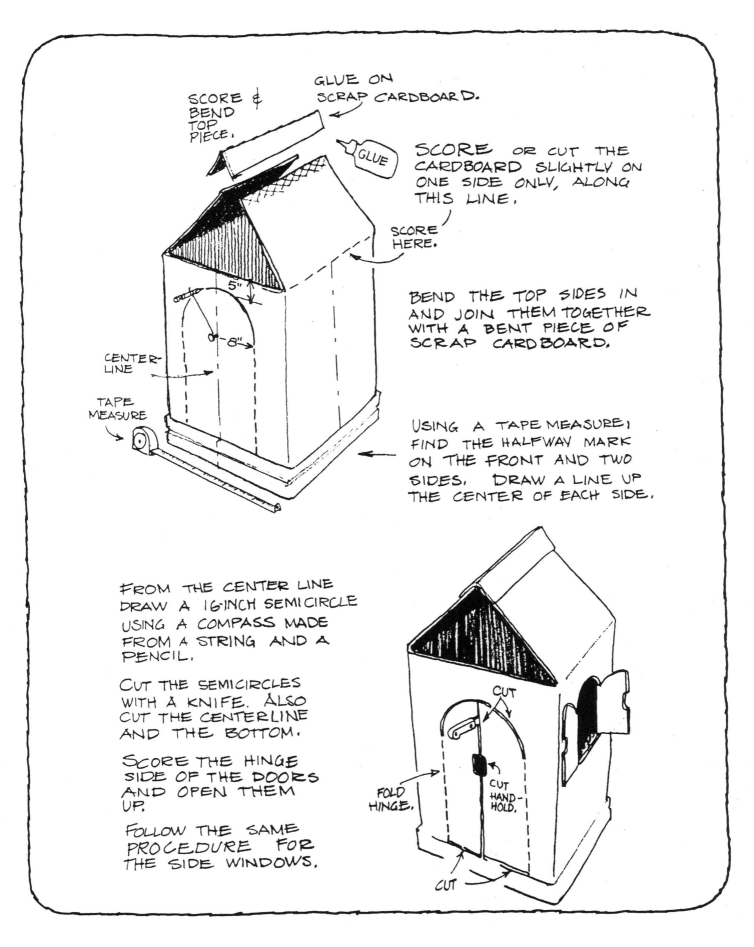

SCORE & BEND TOP PIECE.

GLUE ON SCRAP CARDBOARD.

SCORE or CUT THE CARDBOARD SLIGHTLY ON ONE SIDE ONLY, ALONG THIS LINE.

SCORE HERE.

GLUE

5"

8"

CENTER LINE

TAPE MEASURE

BEND THE TOP SIDES IN AND JOIN THEM TOGETHER WITH A BENT PIECE OF SCRAP CARDBOARD.

USING A TAPE MEASURE, FIND THE HALFWAY MARK ON THE FRONT AND TWO SIDES. DRAW A LINE UP THE CENTER OF EACH SIDE.

FROM THE CENTER LINE DRAW A 16-INCH SEMICIRCLE USING A COMPASS MADE FROM A STRING AND A PENCIL.

CUT THE SEMICIRCLES WITH A KNIFE. ALSO CUT THE CENTERLINE AND THE BOTTOM.

SCORE THE HINGE SIDE OF THE DOORS AND OPEN THEM UP.

FOLLOW THE SAME PROCEDURE FOR THE SIDE WINDOWS.

CUT

FOLD HINGE.

CUT HAND-HOLD.

CUT

THIS FORT IS MADE ENTIRELY OF CARDBOARD BOXES FOUND AT SUPER-MARKETS AND LIQUOR STORES. SOME CARDBOARD BOXES ARE SO STRONG THAT THEY CAN SUPPORT A LARGE MAN.

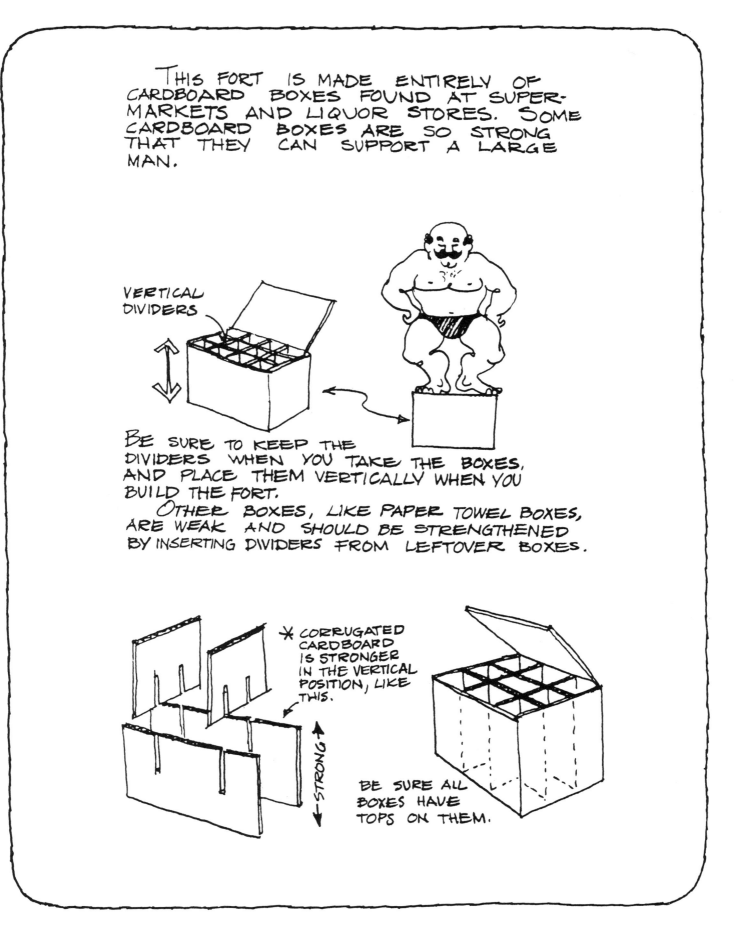

VERTICAL DIVIDERS

BE SURE TO KEEP THE DIVIDERS WHEN YOU TAKE THE BOXES, AND PLACE THEM VERTICALLY WHEN YOU BUILD THE FORT.

OTHER BOXES, LIKE PAPER TOWEL BOXES, ARE WEAK AND SHOULD BE STRENGTHENED BY INSERTING DIVIDERS FROM LEFTOVER BOXES.

* CORRUGATED CARDBOARD IS STRONGER IN THE VERTICAL POSITION, LIKE THIS.

← STRONG →

BE SURE ALL BOXES HAVE TOPS ON THEM.

TOOLS YOU WILL NEED:

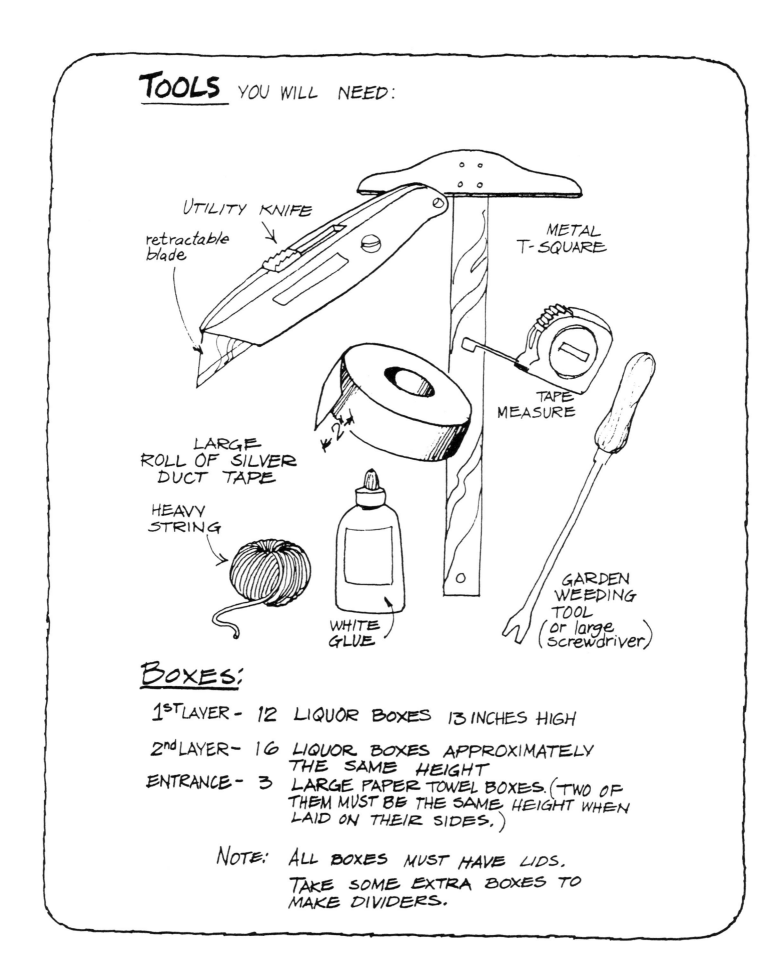

UTILITY KNIFE

retractable blade

METAL T-SQUARE

TAPE MEASURE

LARGE ROLL OF SILVER DUCT TAPE

HEAVY STRING

WHITE GLUE

GARDEN WEEDING TOOL (or large screwdriver)

BOXES:

1ST LAYER — 12 LIQUOR BOXES 13 INCHES HIGH

2nd LAYER — 16 LIQUOR BOXES APPROXIMATELY THE SAME HEIGHT

ENTRANCE — 3 LARGE PAPER TOWEL BOXES. (TWO OF THEM MUST BE THE SAME HEIGHT WHEN LAID ON THEIR SIDES.)

NOTE: ALL BOXES MUST HAVE LIDS.

TAKE SOME EXTRA BOXES TO MAKE DIVIDERS.

BEGIN BY MEASURING ALL THE LIQUOR BOXES AND FIND 12 THAT ARE THE SAME HEIGHT.

ARRANGE THE BOXES IN AN OPEN CIRCLE WITH THEIR LIDS POINTING OUT FROM THE CENTER OF THE CIRCLE.

TAKE TWO PAPER TOWEL BOXES AND REINFORCE THEM WITH CARDBOARD DIVIDERS. SET THEM IN FRONT OF THE OPEN CIRCLE TO FORM AN ENTRANCE AND PLACE A THIRD LARGE BOX ON TOP.

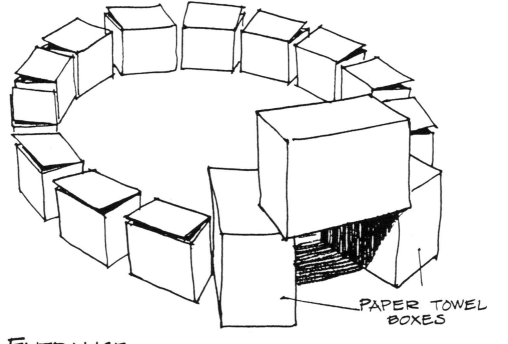

PAPER TOWEL BOXES

ENTRANCE

THE ENTRANCE BOXES ARE JOINED BY LACING THEM TOGETHER WITH HEAVY STRING. USING A WEEDING TOOL OR LARGE SCREWDRIVER, POKE HOLES THROUGH THE BOTTOM AND TOP BOXES. LACE A SHORT LOOP OF STRING THROUGH THE HOLES AND TIE THE BOXES TOGETHER.

(SEE ILLUSTRATION ON NEXT PAGE.)

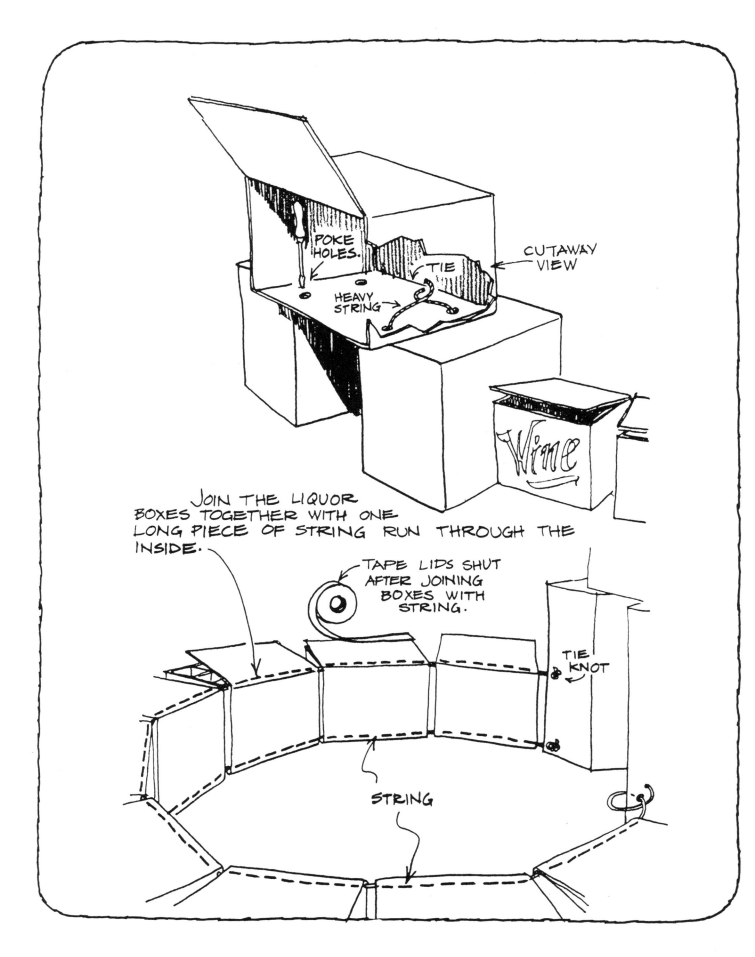

POKE HOLES.

CUTAWAY VIEW

TIE

HEAVY STRING

Wine

JOIN THE LIQUOR BOXES TOGETHER WITH ONE LONG PIECE OF STRING RUN THROUGH THE INSIDE.

TAPE LIDS SHUT AFTER JOINING BOXES WITH STRING.

TIE KNOT

STRING

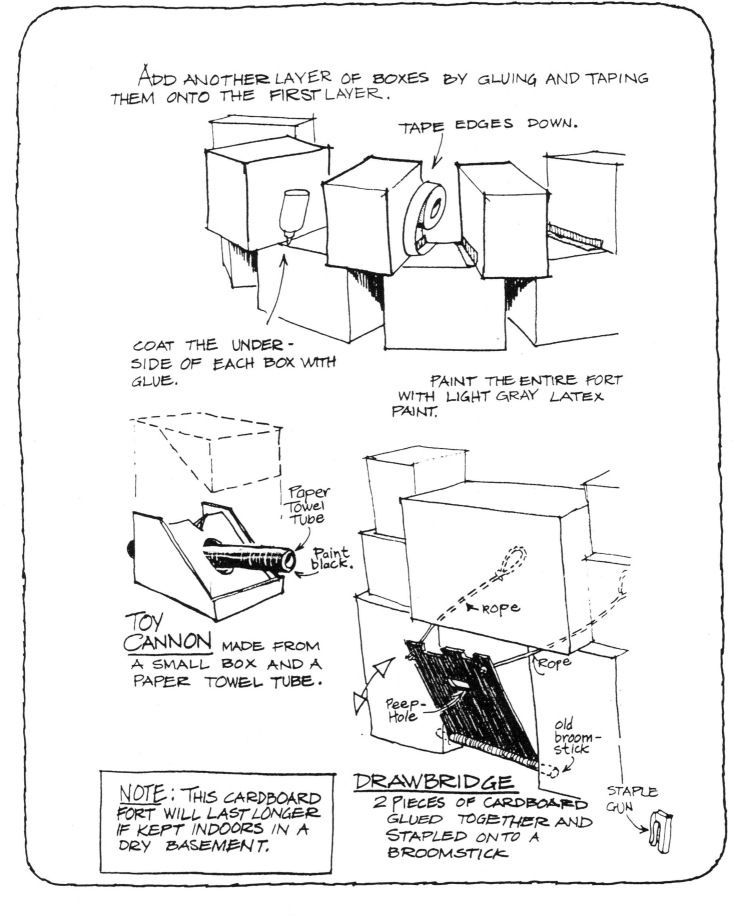

ADD ANOTHER LAYER OF BOXES BY GLUING AND TAPING THEM ONTO THE FIRST LAYER.

TAPE EDGES DOWN.

COAT THE UNDER-SIDE OF EACH BOX WITH GLUE.

PAINT THE ENTIRE FORT WITH LIGHT GRAY LATEX PAINT.

Paper Towel Tube

Paint black.

TOY CANNON MADE FROM A SMALL BOX AND A PAPER TOWEL TUBE.

Rope

Rope

Peep-Hole

old broom-stick

STAPLE GUN

NOTE: THIS CARDBOARD FORT WILL LAST LONGER IF KEPT INDOORS IN A DRY BASEMENT.

DRAWBRIDGE
2 PIECES OF CARDBOARD GLUED TOGETHER AND STAPLED ONTO A BROOMSTICK

SAND FORTS CAN BE MADE QUITE EASILY IF YOU REMEMBER TO BRING THE PROPER EQUIPMENT WITH YOU TO THE BEACH. SOME OF THE THINGS YOU MIGHT NEED ARE:

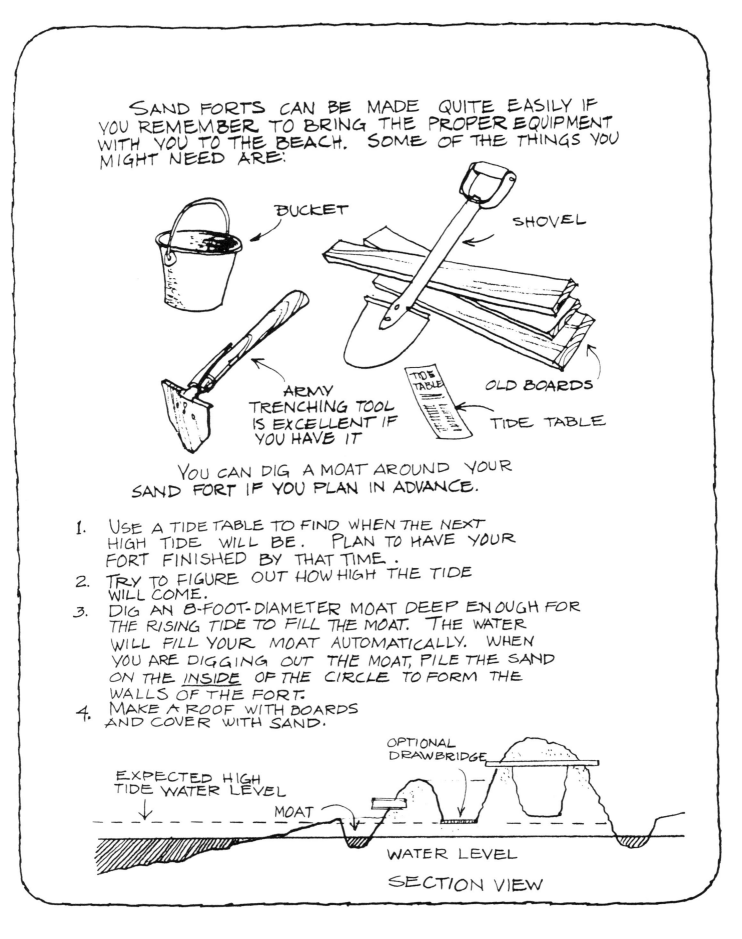

BUCKET

SHOVEL

OLD BOARDS

ARMY TRENCHING TOOL IS EXCELLENT IF YOU HAVE IT

TIDE TABLE

YOU CAN DIG A MOAT AROUND YOUR SAND FORT IF YOU PLAN IN ADVANCE.

1. USE A TIDE TABLE TO FIND WHEN THE NEXT HIGH TIDE WILL BE. PLAN TO HAVE YOUR FORT FINISHED BY THAT TIME.
2. TRY TO FIGURE OUT HOW HIGH THE TIDE WILL COME.
3. DIG AN 8-FOOT-DIAMETER MOAT DEEP ENOUGH FOR THE RISING TIDE TO FILL THE MOAT. THE WATER WILL FILL YOUR MOAT AUTOMATICALLY. WHEN YOU ARE DIGGING OUT THE MOAT, PILE THE SAND ON THE <u>INSIDE</u> OF THE CIRCLE TO FORM THE WALLS OF THE FORT.
4. MAKE A ROOF WITH BOARDS AND COVER WITH SAND.

OPTIONAL DRAWBRIDGE

EXPECTED HIGH TIDE WATER LEVEL

MOAT

WATER LEVEL

SECTION VIEW

LEAF FORT

FIND THREE LONG BRANCHES AND TIE THE ENDS TOGETHER WITH ROPE OR WIRE. SPREAD OUT THE BRANCHES. TIE ANOTHER BRANCH ACROSS TWO OF THE BRANCHES TO FRAME THE DOOR.

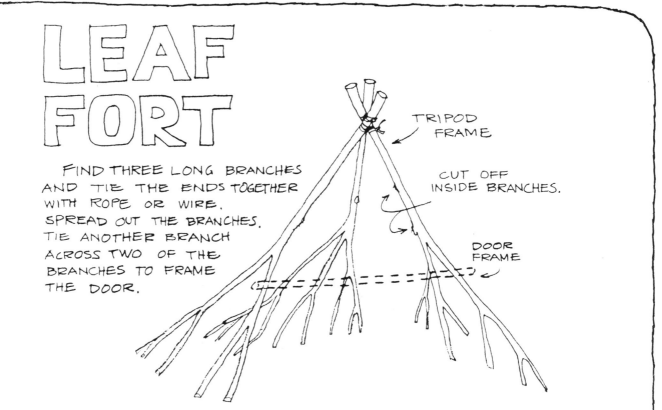

TRIPOD FRAME

CUT OFF INSIDE BRANCHES.

DOOR FRAME

THEN PILE UP ALL THE BRANCHES YOU CAN FIND, STARTING WITH BIG ONES AND FINISHING WITH SMALL ONES. TRY TO WEAVE SMALLER BRANCHES IN AND OUT OF THE LARGER BRANCHES TO FORM AN ENCLOSURE.

PILE UP LOTS AND LOTS OF LEAVES. NOW YOUR LEAF FORT IS CAMOUFLAGED AND READY FOR ACTION.

GREAT SECRET HIDING PLACE!

SNOW-BALL FORT

SNOWBALL FORTS ARE MADE BY ROLLING BIG BALLS OF SNOW TO ONE LOCATION AND PILING THEM ON TOP OF EACH OTHER TO FORM A FORT. BOARDS PLACED ACROSS THE TOP FORM THE ROOF, AND A SECOND WALL IN FRONT OF THE MAIN STRUCTURE FORMS A PROTECTIVE BARRIER AGAINST ATTACK. BE SURE TO PROVIDE SMALL WINDOWS AROUND THE FORT SO YOU CAN OBSERVE POTENTIAL INVADERS. BUILD A SMALL LEDGE ON THE INSIDE OF THE WALL TO HOLD SNOWBALLS IN READINESS AND HAVE AN EXTRA SUPPLY IN AN AMMUNITION SLED MADE OUT OF AN OLD WOODEN FRUIT BOX.

FRUIT

1×4

AMMUNITION SLED

SNOW BLOCK FORT

THE SNOW-BLOCK FORT IS BUILT USING A MOLD THAT YOU MAKE OUT OF A BOX. THE BOX IS $\frac{1}{2}$-INCH PLYWOOD, NAILED TOGETHER WITH $1\frac{1}{2}$-INCH FINISHING NAILS AND VARNISHED. TO BUILD THE FORT, PACK THE BOX WITH SNOW AND DRAG IT TO THE FORT SITE. TURN THE BOX UPSIDE DOWN, STACK UP THE BLOCKS, AND MAKE A CIRCULAR FORT.

$1\frac{1}{2}$" HOLE

12"

5"

10"

13"

16"

SNOW MOLD BOX

CITY SNOW FORT

Lucky are you if you live in the city during a heavy snowstorm. Wait for the snowplow to finish clearing the streets and look for a large pile where they have deposited their load of snow. Place three or four boards across the top, shovel out the snow from underneath, and pile it on top. In no time at all, you will have a snow fort.

Ask your mom and dad for help, to make sure that you are building your fort in a safe place out of the path of cars.

SNÖ-HUS

A SIMPLER VERSION OF THE ESKIMO SNOW HOUSE IS THIS SNÖ-HUS RECOMMENDED BY ANIKA BERNHARD, WHO BUILT THEM WHEN SHE WAS A LITTLE GIRL IN SWEDEN.

WITH THE HELP OF SOME FRIENDS, PILE UP AS MUCH SNOW AS YOU CAN INTO A BEEHIVE-SHAPED MOUND. USE TOBOGGANS, SLEDS, OR WHATEVER YOU CAN FIND TO CARRY ADDITIONAL SNOW TO YOUR BUILDING SITE. THE LAST 8 TO 12 INCHES OF SNOW SURFACE SHOULD BE PACKED SOLID WITH NO HOLES. WHEN THE SNOW MOUND IS FINISHED, WAIT FOR A COLD NIGHT AND SPRINKLE THE ENTIRE SURFACE WITH WATER FROM A WATERING CAN. WHEN THE OUTSIDE SURFACE HAS FROZEN SOLID, CUT A HOLE FOR A DOOR AND REMOVE THE SNOW FROM THE INSIDE UNTIL THE WALLS ARE 1½ FEET THICK AT THE BOTTOM AND 10 INCHES THICK AT THE TOP. CUT A SMALL (1 INCH) SMOKE HOLE IN THE TOP AND LIGHT A SMALL FIRE IN THE HUT. ALLOW THE FIRE TO BURN UNTIL THE CEILING IS NOTICEABLY WET, AND THEN EXTINGUISH THE FLAME. ASK MOM AND DAD TO HELP YOU WITH THIS.

ALLOW THE INTERIOR TO FREEZE OVER, AND YOU WILL HAVE A HARD SURFACE BOTH INSIDE AND OUT WITH SOFT SNOW IN THE MIDDLE ACTING AS AN INSULATOR.

BUILD UP THE FLOOR WITH 6 TO 8 INCHES OF EVERGREEN BOUGHS AND TWIGS, AND COVER THEM WITH AN OLD RUG OR A HEAVY TARP. THIS IS TO KEEP YOUR BODY HEAT FROM MELTING THE FLOOR AS MUCH AS IT IS TO KEEP THE FLOOR FROM FREEZING YOU.

CONSTRUCT A BED PLATFORM SO THAT YOU ARE SLEEPING <u>HIGHER</u> THAN THE TOP OF THE DOOR OPENING.

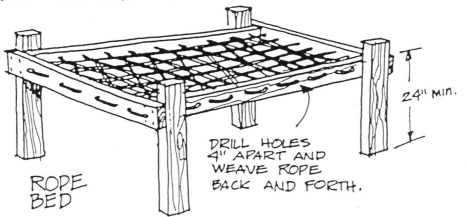

ROPE BED

24" MIN.

DRILL HOLES 4" APART AND WEAVE ROPE BACK AND FORTH.

THE ENTRANCE CAN BE MADE FROM A WOODEN PACKING CRATE OR SCRAPS OF WOOD. MAKE A DOOR AT EACH END TO KEEP OUT DRAFTS.

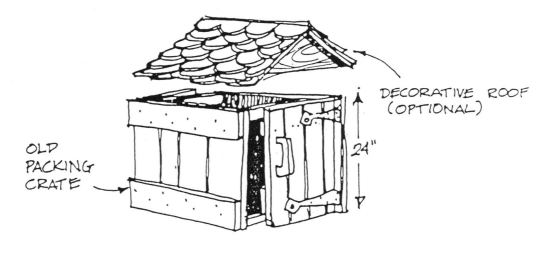

DECORATIVE ROOF (OPTIONAL)

OLD PACKING CRATE

24"

A SEMI-TRANSPARENT WINDOW CAN BE MADE BY FREEZING SOME WATER IN A SQUARE BAKING DISH AND WEDGING THE ICE INTO AN OPENING OF THE SAME SIZE CUT INTO THE WALL.

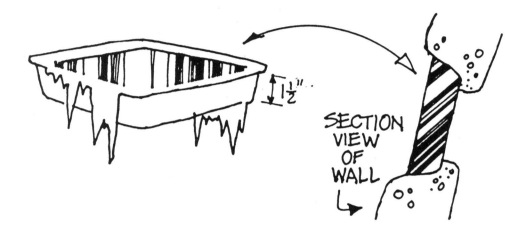

SECTION VIEW OF WALL

FOR THE MORE AMBITIOUS BUILDER, SEVERAL DOMED ROOMS CAN BE ADDED BY CONNECTING TUNNELS OR INTERSECTING DOMES.

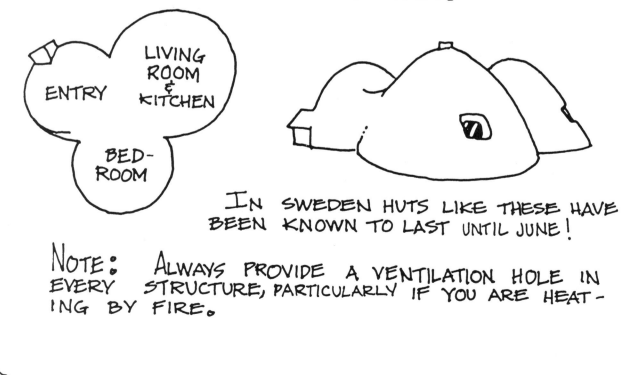

ENTRY

LIVING ROOM & KITCHEN

BED-ROOM

IN SWEDEN HUTS LIKE THESE HAVE BEEN KNOWN TO LAST UNTIL JUNE!

NOTE: ALWAYS PROVIDE A VENTILATION HOLE IN EVERY STRUCTURE, PARTICULARLY IF YOU ARE HEATING BY FIRE.

Snö Lykta

(SNOW LIGHT)

The object that you see outside the door of the snö-hus is a "snö lykta" (snow light). The Swedish custom is to have a snö lykta outside one's house as an expression of good cheer.

The snö lyktas often become elaborate sculptures. The main idea is to have an enclosure for a candle so that the flame sends a warm glow through the snow, out into the night.

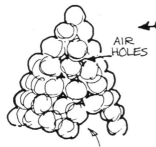

AIR HOLES

HOLE IN BASE FOR CANDLE

The simplest way is to build a pyramid of snowballs, hollow on the inside, and place a candle inside ...

... or a more elaborate one can be made by forming it solid first and carving it out with a knife.

Another version, dating back to the early 1900s, as told by Ma Karlstrom, was made this way:

FILL A PAIL WITH WATER AND ALLOW THE INSIDE SURFACE TO PARTIALLY FREEZE.

REMOVE THE PAIL AND CUT A HOLE IN THE BOTTOM. LET THE WATER OUT.

PROVIDE AN AIR HOLE IN THE BOTTOM FOR THE CANDLE.

Note: The following three forts involve some complicated instructions and carpentry. Ask your parents for help.

BUNKER FORT

Structures like this have been built for centuries by shepherds, vineyard workers, and farmers all over the world. During wartime they were used as observation posts and gun installations due to their solid construction and because they were difficult for the enemy to observe.

Built almost entirely from materials found in the woods, the bunker provides adequate shelter at minimum cost.

During the winter the bunker can be closed up in front to provide a warm place to sleep.

Find a secluded spot with a terrific view, preferably on a hilltop. Begin by digging out the side of the hill and piling the dirt in front.

Dig out an area 5-feet square for the bunker and provide a 4-foot flat area in front.

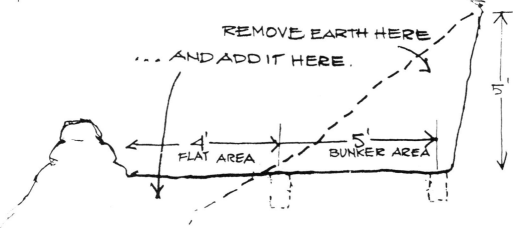

REMOVE EARTH HERE

... AND ADD IT HERE.

4'
FLAT AREA

5'
BUNKER AREA

5'

Find four heavy forked branches in the woods and cut them 5-feet long. Dig four 12-inch-deep holes in a square 5-feet apart and bury the poles in the ground.

5'   5'

- Lay a crossbeam across each pair of posts.

- Next, build a rear wall behind the back posts with boards or logs.

- Build the side walls in the same manner. When you have built the walls 12 inches high, stop and lay some floorboards across, then continue the wall to the top.

Next, find a fat log for the ridgepole. Lay it front-to-rear on the two crossbeams, then cover the roof with boards.

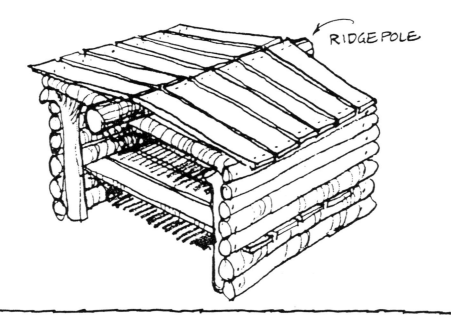

Starting from the bottom, staple tar paper over the outside walls and roof.

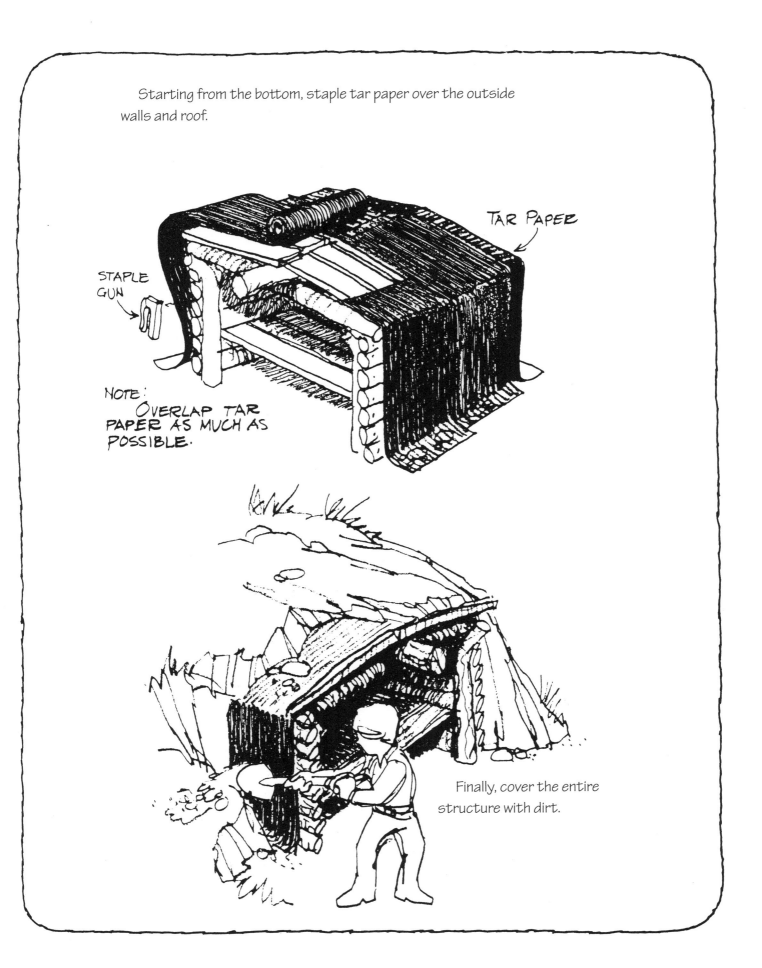

TAR PAPER

STAPLE GUN

NOTE:
OVERLAP TAR PAPER AS MUCH AS POSSIBLE.

Finally, cover the entire structure with dirt.

FIND THREE TREES 6 TO 8 FEET APART IN A TRIANGLE. THEY SHOULD BE ALIVE AND AT LEAST 6" THICK. NAIL 2X6 BEAMS AROUND THE OUTSIDE OF THE TREES TO HOLD THE FLOOR AND THE ROOF. MAKE SURE THE FLOOR IS LEVEL. THE ROOF SHOULD SLANT BACK DOWN A FEW INCHES TO ALLOW THE RAIN TO RUN OFF.

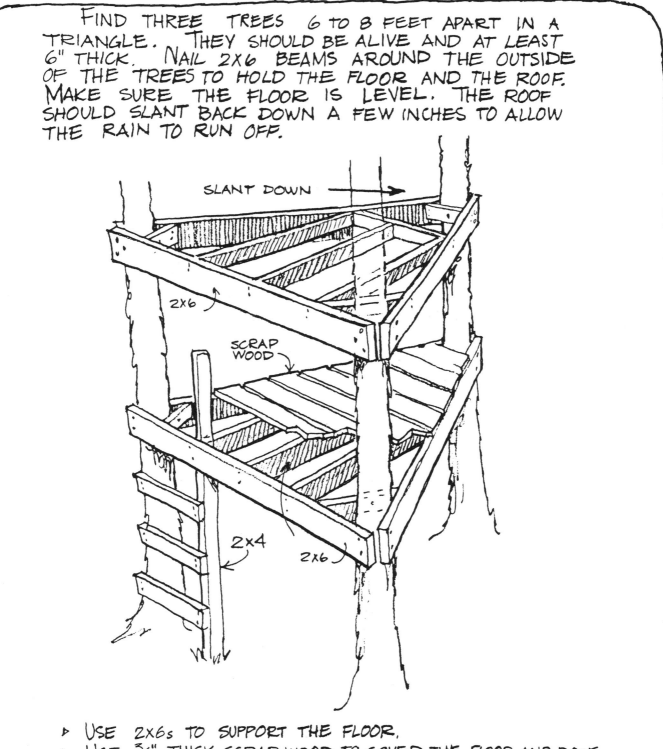

▷ USE 2X6s TO SUPPORT THE FLOOR.
▷ USE ¾"-THICK SCRAP WOOD TO COVER THE FLOOR AND ROOF.
▷ USE 2X4s TO MAKE THE RAILINGS AND THE LADDER.
▷ USE ONLY GALVANIZED COATED NAILS AND ⅝" LAG SCREWS.
▷ COVER THE ROOF WITH ASPHALT SHINGLES.
▷ YOU MAY NEED THE HELP OF AN ADULT.

45

SPACE STATION FORT

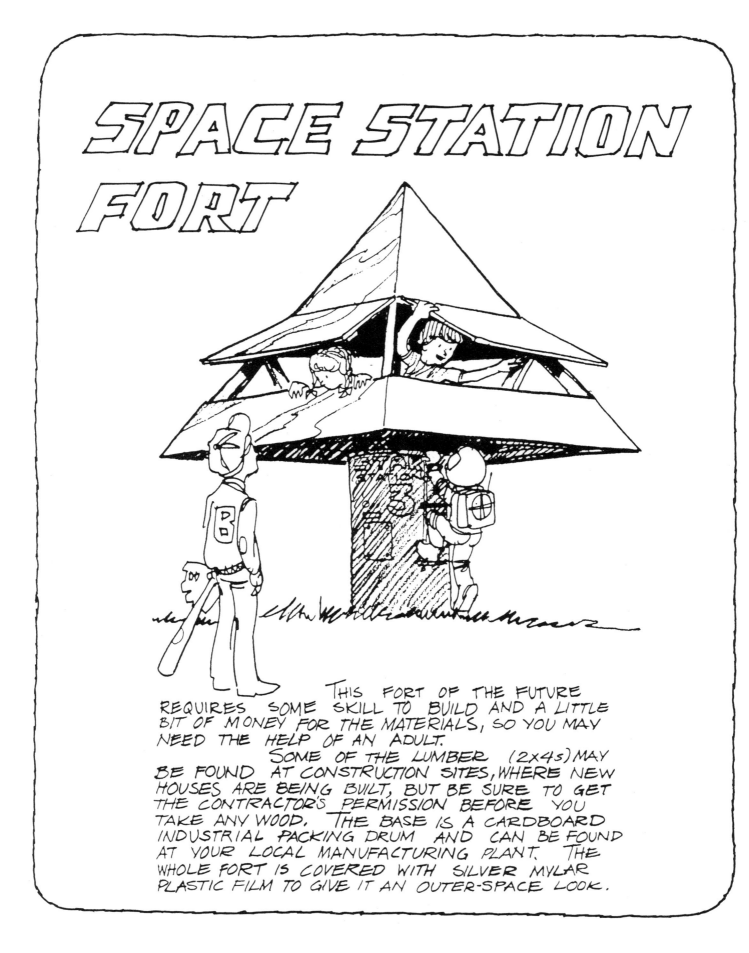

This fort of the future requires some skill to build and a little bit of money for the materials, so you may need the help of an adult.

Some of the lumber (2x4s) may be found at construction sites, where new houses are being built, but be sure to get the contractor's permission before you take any wood. The base is a cardboard industrial packing drum and can be found at your local manufacturing plant. The whole fort is covered with silver mylar plastic film to give it an outer-space look.

Materials

FOUR	4×4	6' LONG	POSTS
FOUR	2×4	8' 6" LONG	CROSS BEAMS
FOUR	2×4	6' LONG	FLOOR PERIMETER FRAME
FOUR	2×4	7'4" LONG	DIAGONAL UPRIGHTS
FOUR	2×4	4'6" LONG	LOWER WINDOW FRAME
FOUR	2×4	28" LONG	UPPER WINDOW FRAME
FOUR	1×3	4'6" LONG	WINDOW STIFFENERS
FOUR	2×3	1' LONG	WINDOW PROPS
ONE	$\frac{1}{2}$"	PLYWOOD 4'×8' *	FLOOR
FOUR	$\frac{1}{2}$" CDX PLYWOOD 4'×8' *		SIDES
ONE	32" high 20"DIAMETER PAPER PACKING DRUM – BASE		
FOUR	SETS 2" BUTT HINGES		WINDOW HINGES
ONE	ROLL REFLECTIVE MYLAR 30'×5' COVERING		

* THIS IS WHAT YOU ASK FOR AT THE LUMBERYARD.

BEFORE YOU BEGIN, IT IS A GOOD IDEA TO DISCUSS THIS PROJECT WITH YOUR NEIGHBORS AND GET THEIR APPROVAL. PERHAPS THEY WILL LEND A HAND OR VOLUNTEER SOME MATERIALS.

FIND A SPOT THAT IS REASONABLY FLAT AND DIG FOUR 24" DEEP HOLES 12" ON CENTER WITH A POSTHOLE DIGGER.

PLACE THE DRUM AROUND THE HOLES AND INSERT THE FOUR POSTS THROUGH THE DRUM AND INTO THE HOLES. BE SURE THE POSTS ARE TOUCHING THE INSIDE WALL OF THE DRUM AND CHECK WITH A LEVEL TO BE SURE THEY ARE VERTICAL. THEN FILL THE POSTHOLES WITH CONCRETE.

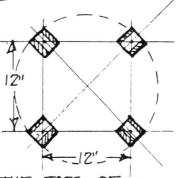

MARK A LEVEL LINE ACROSS THE TOPS OF THE POSTS, EVEN WITH THE TOP OF THE DRUM, AND MAKE A NOTCH ON BOTH SIDES OF EACH POST TO ACCEPT THE CROSSBEAMS.

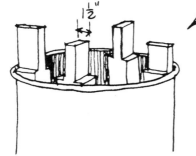

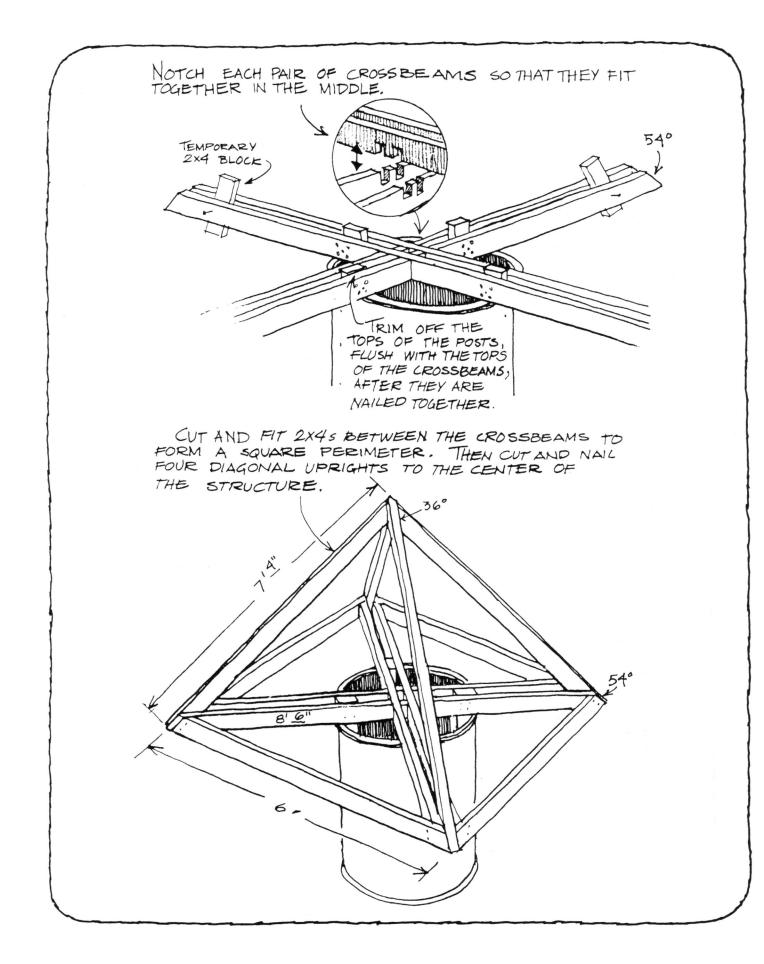

NOTCH EACH PAIR OF CROSSBEAMS SO THAT THEY FIT TOGETHER IN THE MIDDLE.

TEMPORARY 2x4 BLOCK

54°

TRIM OFF THE TOPS OF THE POSTS, FLUSH WITH THE TOPS OF THE CROSSBEAMS, AFTER THEY ARE NAILED TOGETHER.

CUT AND FIT 2x4s BETWEEN THE CROSSBEAMS TO FORM A SQUARE PERIMETER. THEN CUT AND NAIL FOUR DIAGONAL UPRIGHTS TO THE CENTER OF THE STRUCTURE.

36°

7'4"

54°

8' 6"

6'

PLAN VIEW

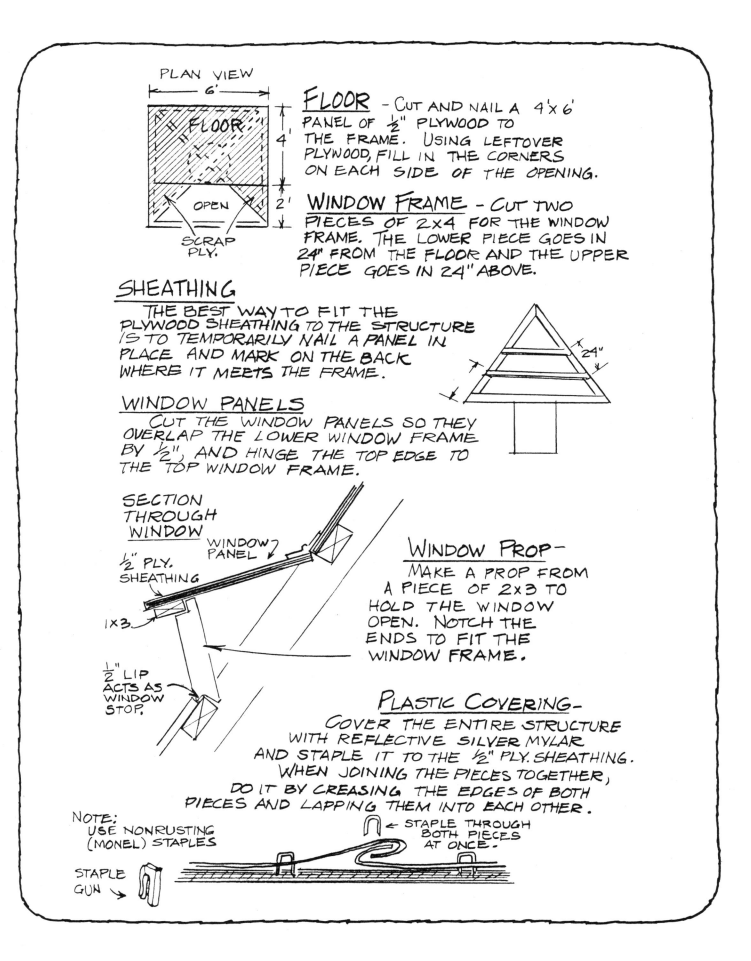

FLOOR – Cut and nail a 4'×6' panel of ½" plywood to the frame. Using leftover plywood, fill in the corners on each side of the opening.

WINDOW FRAME – Cut two pieces of 2×4 for the window frame. The lower piece goes in 24" from the floor and the upper piece goes in 24" above.

SHEATHING

The best way to fit the plywood sheathing to the structure is to temporarily nail a panel in place and mark on the back where it meets the frame.

WINDOW PANELS

Cut the window panels so they overlap the lower window frame by ½", and hinge the top edge to the top window frame.

SECTION THROUGH WINDOW

WINDOW PANEL

½" PLY. SHEATHING

1×3

½" LIP ACTS AS WINDOW STOP.

WINDOW PROP –

Make a prop from a piece of 2×3 to hold the window open. Notch the ends to fit the window frame.

PLASTIC COVERING –

Cover the entire structure with reflective silver mylar and staple it to the ½" ply. sheathing. When joining the pieces together, do it by creasing the edges of both pieces and lapping them into each other.

NOTE:
USE NONRUSTING (MONEL) STAPLES

STAPLE GUN →

← STAPLE THROUGH BOTH PIECES AT ONCE.

Kid-Built Fort

KIDS CAN BUILD THIS FORT
THEMSELVES ONCE THE
POSTS ARE INSTALLED.

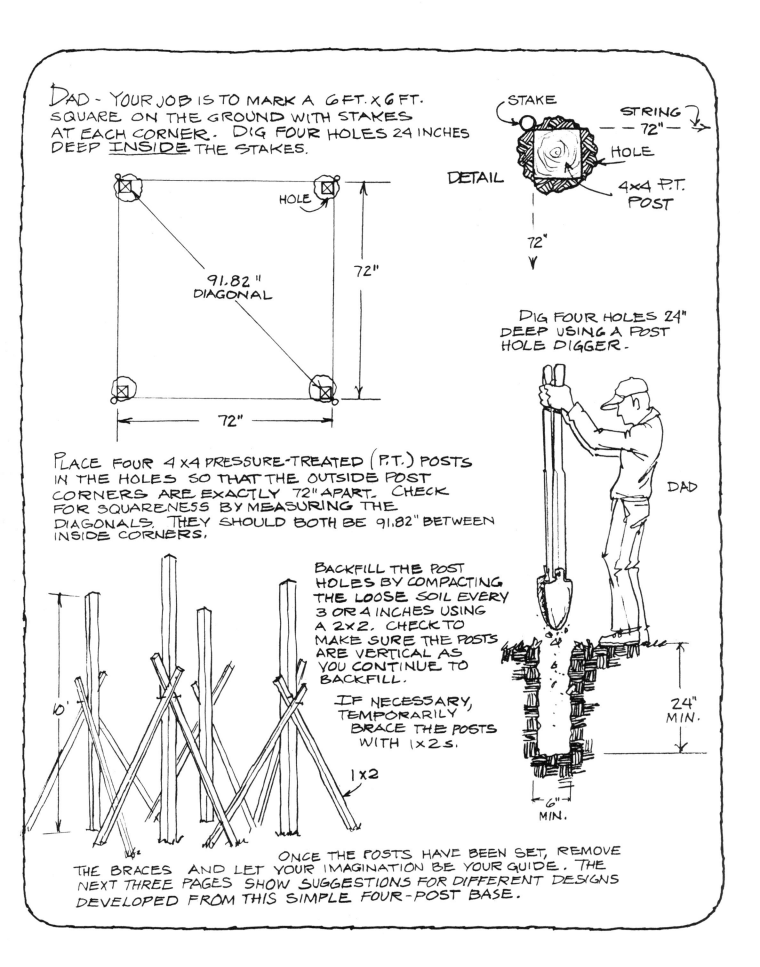

DAD - YOUR JOB IS TO MARK A 6 FT. X 6 FT. SQUARE ON THE GROUND WITH STAKES AT EACH CORNER. DIG FOUR HOLES 24 INCHES DEEP **INSIDE** THE STAKES.

STAKE

STRING
— — 72" — —

HOLE

DETAIL

4×4 P.T. POST

72"

91.82" DIAGONAL

72"

HOLE

72"

DIG FOUR HOLES 24" DEEP USING A POST HOLE DIGGER.

PLACE FOUR 4×4 PRESSURE-TREATED (P.T.) POSTS IN THE HOLES SO THAT THE OUTSIDE POST CORNERS ARE EXACTLY 72" APART. CHECK FOR SQUARENESS BY MEASURING THE DIAGONALS. THEY SHOULD BOTH BE 91.82" BETWEEN INSIDE CORNERS,

BACKFILL THE POST HOLES BY COMPACTING THE LOOSE SOIL EVERY 3 OR 4 INCHES USING A 2×2. CHECK TO MAKE SURE THE POSTS ARE VERTICAL AS YOU CONTINUE TO BACKFILL.

IF NECESSARY, TEMPORARILY BRACE THE POSTS WITH 1×2s.

DAD

10'

1×2

24" MIN.

6" MIN.

ONCE THE POSTS HAVE BEEN SET, REMOVE THE BRACES AND LET YOUR IMAGINATION BE YOUR GUIDE. THE NEXT THREE PAGES SHOW SUGGESTIONS FOR DIFFERENT DESIGNS DEVELOPED FROM THIS SIMPLE FOUR-POST BASE.

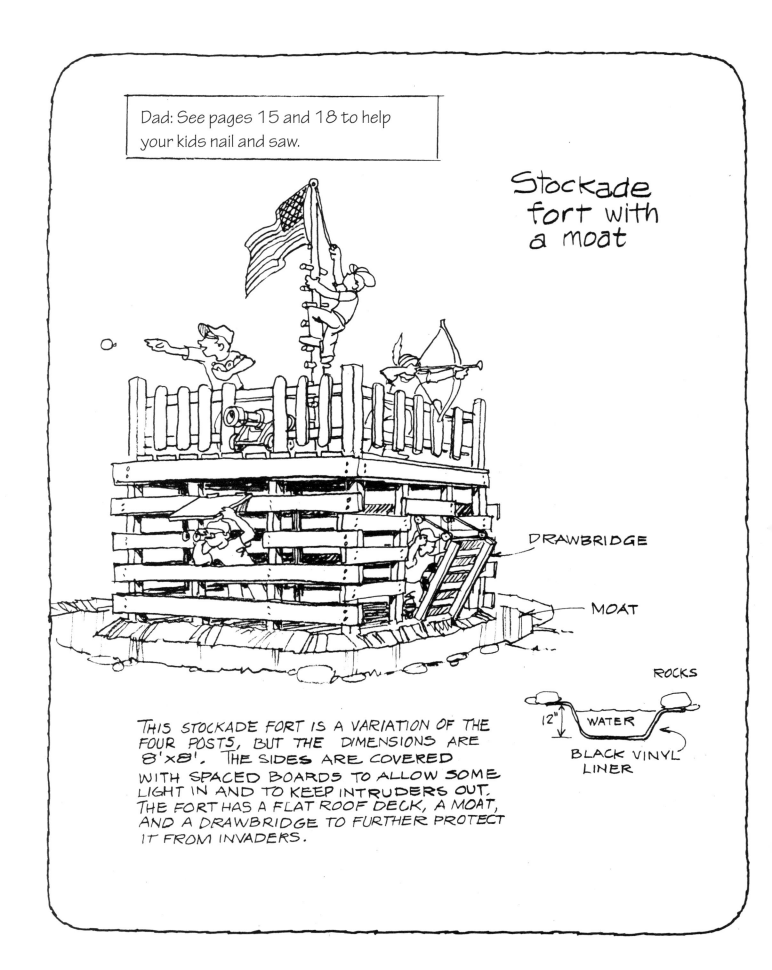

Dad: See pages 15 and 18 to help your kids nail and saw.

Stockade fort with a moat

DRAWBRIDGE

MOAT

ROCKS

12" WATER

BLACK VINYL LINER

THIS STOCKADE FORT IS A VARIATION OF THE FOUR POSTS, BUT THE DIMENSIONS ARE 8'×8'. THE SIDES ARE COVERED WITH SPACED BOARDS TO ALLOW SOME LIGHT IN AND TO KEEP INTRUDERS OUT. THE FORT HAS A FLAT ROOF DECK, A MOAT, AND A DRAWBRIDGE TO FURTHER PROTECT IT FROM INVADERS.

A covered fort with a slide

WITH A LITTLE HELP FROM MOM AND DAD, A ROOF CAN BE ADDED AND PERHAPS A SLIDE.

2x4 RAFTERS

1x6 RIDGE

4'x8' x ½" PLYWOOD

2x6

45°

2x6

12"

ROOF - TWO SHEETS OF 4'x8' PLYWOOD

4'

SAND BOX

SLIDE

RAMP

6'

6'

A Blockhouse
(as shown on the cover of this book)

YOU MAY BE FORTUNATE TO FIND THREE OR FOUR TREES GROWING CLOSE TOGETHER, ALLOWING YOU TO AVOID INSTALLING POSTS. IF ONLY TWO OR THREE TREES ARE AVAILABLE, ADD THE POSTS AS DESCRIBED ON PAGE 51.

* Blockhouse - "A fortified structure with ports or loopholes through which defenders may direct gunfire"

RANDOM HOUSE DICTIONARY

STILES/09

Mini-Fort

This mini-fort can be built in just one weekend. It uses nine pieces of 3/4" plywood and eight pieces of 2 x 4, eight feet long. The leftover plywood is used to make the faux (fake) stone facing.

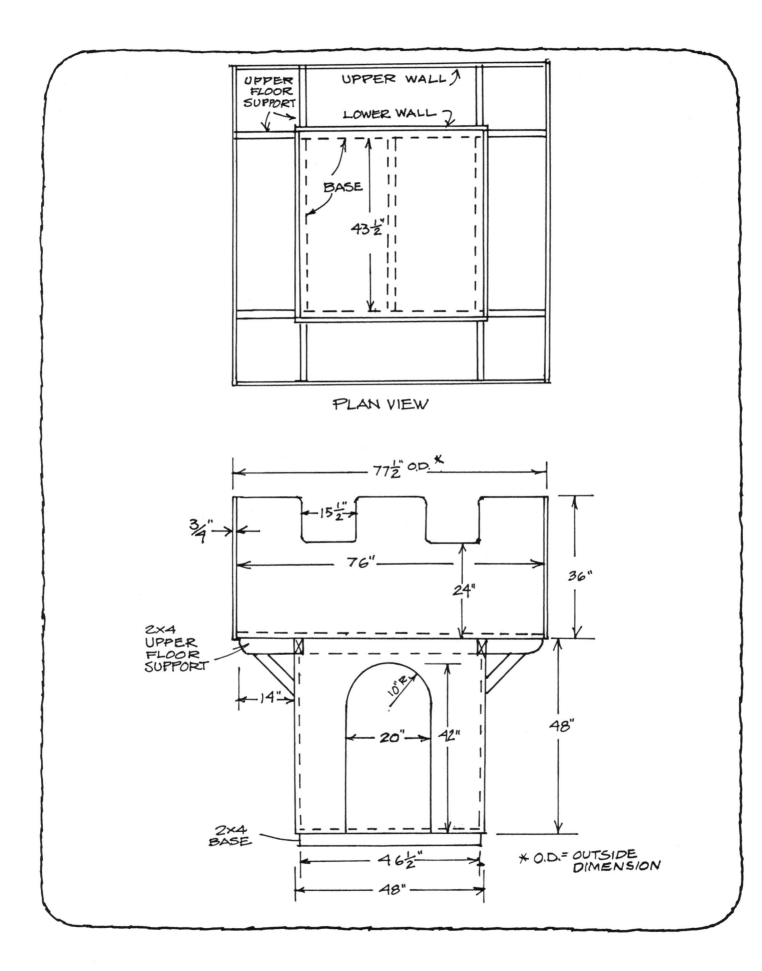

UPPER FLOOR SUPPORT

UPPER WALL ↑

LOWER WALL ↵

BASE

$43\frac{1}{2}"$

PLAN VIEW

$77\frac{1}{2}"$ O.D. *

$15\frac{1}{2}"$

$\frac{3}{4}"$

76"

24"

36"

2×4 UPPER FLOOR SUPPORT

14"

10"R.

20"

42"

48"

2×4 BASE

$46\frac{1}{2}"$

48"

* O.D.= OUTSIDE DIMENSION

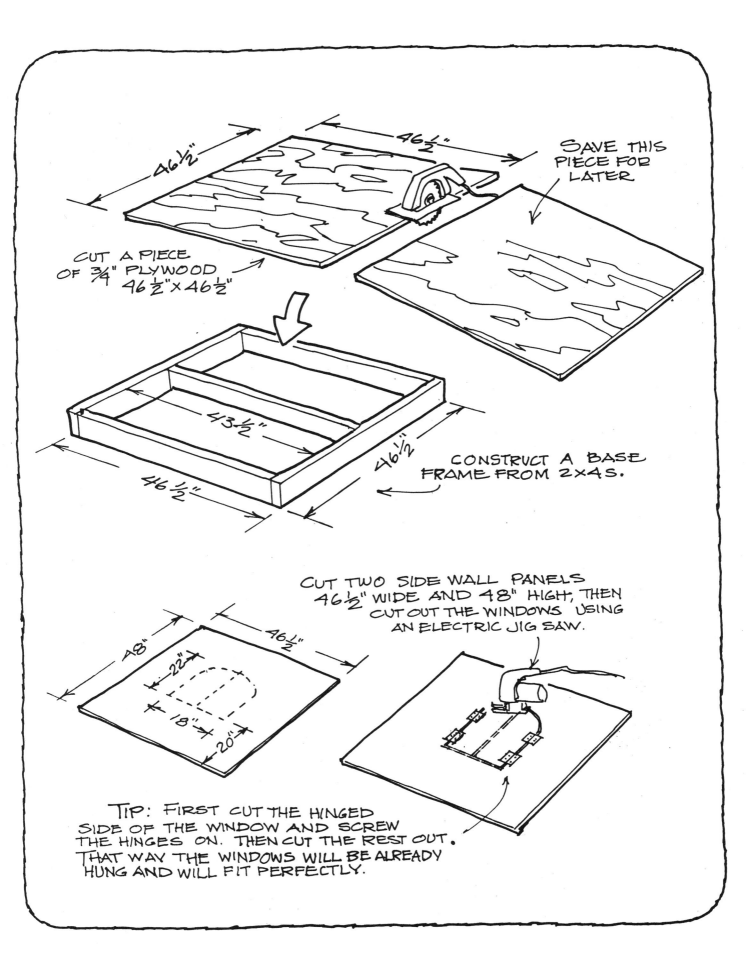

CUT A PIECE OF 3/4" PLYWOOD 46½" X 46½"

46½"

46½"

SAVE THIS PIECE FOR LATER

CONSTRUCT A BASE FRAME FROM 2x4s.

43½"

46½"

46½"

46½"

CUT TWO SIDE WALL PANELS 46½" WIDE AND 48" HIGH, THEN CUT OUT THE WINDOWS USING AN ELECTRIC JIG SAW.

48"

46½"

22"

18"

20"

TIP: FIRST CUT THE HINGED SIDE OF THE WINDOW AND SCREW THE HINGES ON. THEN CUT THE REST OUT. THAT WAY THE WINDOWS WILL BE ALREADY HUNG AND WILL FIT PERFECTLY.

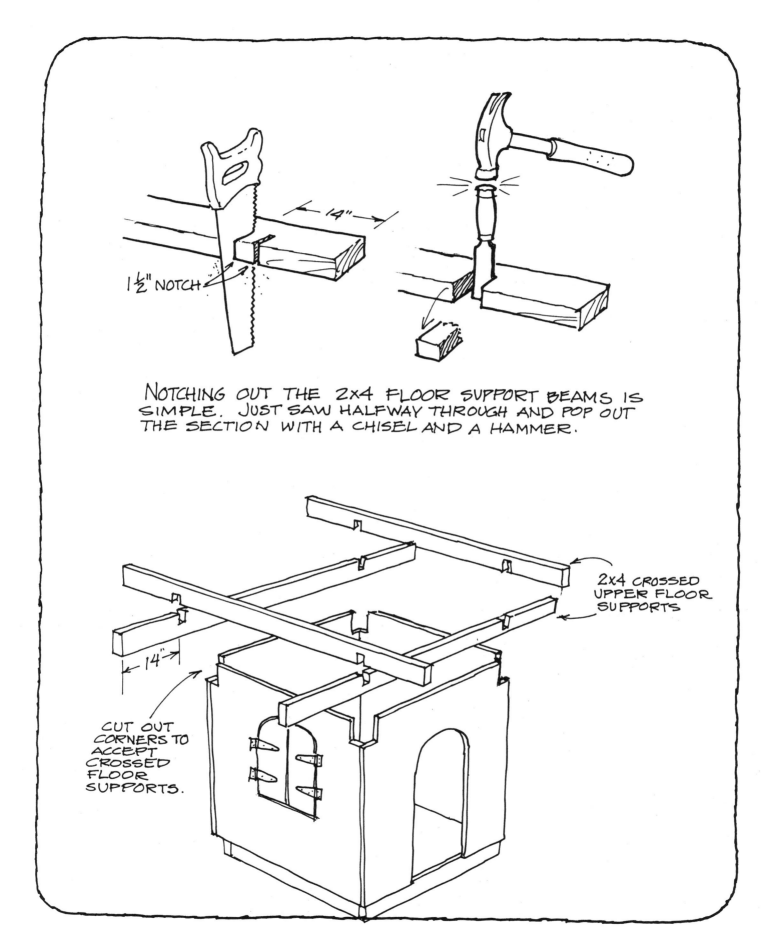

1½" NOTCH

14"

NOTCHING OUT THE 2X4 FLOOR SUPPORT BEAMS IS SIMPLE. JUST SAW HALFWAY THROUGH AND POP OUT THE SECTION WITH A CHISEL AND A HAMMER.

2X4 CROSSED UPPER FLOOR SUPPORTS

14"

CUT OUT CORNERS TO ACCEPT CROSSED FLOOR SUPPORTS.

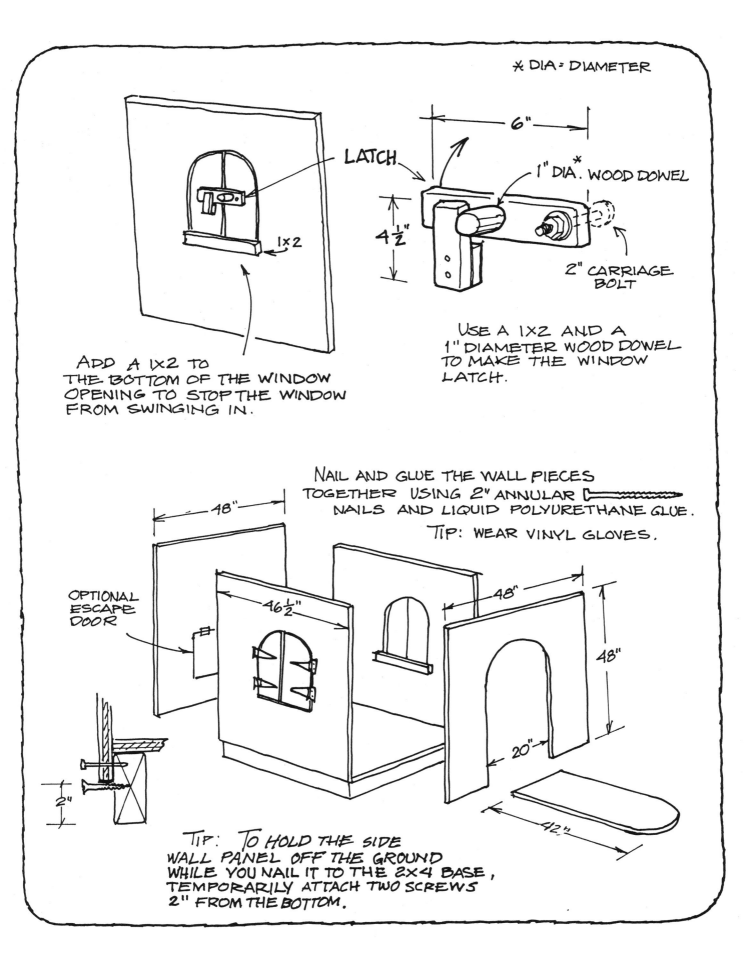

✳ DIA = DIAMETER

LATCH

6"

1" DIA.✳ WOOD DOWEL

4½"

2" CARRIAGE BOLT

ADD A 1X2 TO THE BOTTOM OF THE WINDOW OPENING TO STOP THE WINDOW FROM SWINGING IN.

1X2

USE A 1X2 AND A 1" DIAMETER WOOD DOWEL TO MAKE THE WINDOW LATCH.

NAIL AND GLUE THE WALL PIECES TOGETHER USING 2" ANNULAR NAILS AND LIQUID POLYURETHANE GLUE.

TIP: WEAR VINYL GLOVES.

48"

OPTIONAL ESCAPE DOOR

46½"

48"

48"

20"

2"

42"

TIP: TO HOLD THE SIDE WALL PANEL OFF THE GROUND WHILE YOU NAIL IT TO THE 2X4 BASE, TEMPORARILY ATTACH TWO SCREWS 2" FROM THE BOTTOM.

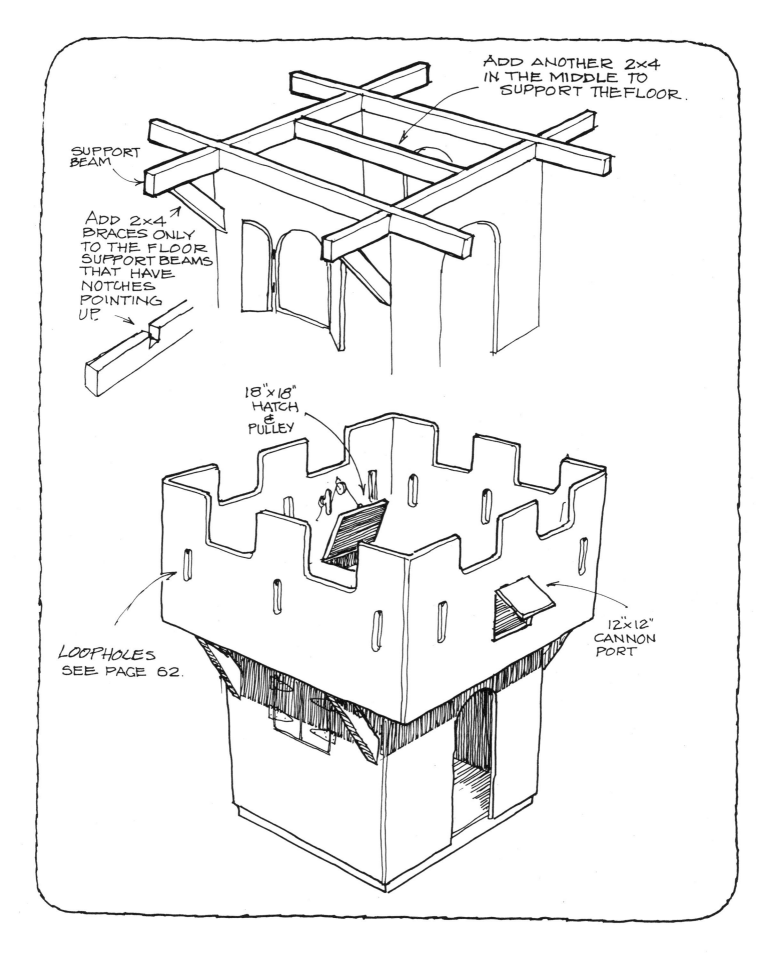

ADD ANOTHER 2×4 IN THE MIDDLE TO SUPPORT THE FLOOR.

SUPPORT BEAM

ADD 2×4 BRACES ONLY TO THE FLOOR SUPPORT BEAMS THAT HAVE NOTCHES POINTING UP.

18"×18" HATCH & PULLEY

LOOPHOLES SEE PAGE 62.

12"×12" CANNON PORT

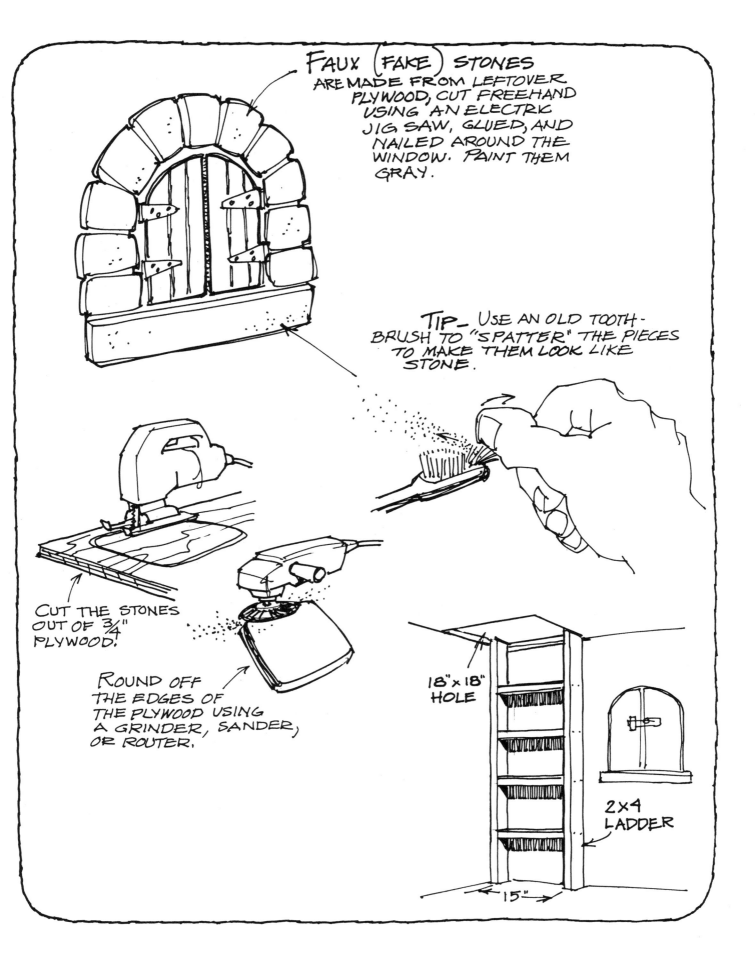

FAUX (FAKE) STONES ARE MADE FROM LEFTOVER PLYWOOD, CUT FREEHAND USING AN ELECTRK JIG SAW, GLUED, AND NAILED AROUND THE WINDOW. PAINT THEM GRAY.

TIP— USE AN OLD TOOTH-BRUSH TO "SPATTER" THE PIECES TO MAKE THEM LOOK LIKE STONE.

CUT THE STONES OUT OF 3/4" PLYWOOD.

ROUND OFF THE EDGES OF THE PLYWOOD USING A GRINDER, SANDER, OR ROUTER.

18" x 18" HOLE

2×4 LADDER

15"

61

Fort Edward

This fort is a combination of an American stockade and an English crusader's fort, with a moat going around the base. The drawbridge is lowered by means of a crank situated above the gatehouse. There are plenty of loopholes (openings in the wall for shooting water guns at unsuspecting invaders) and a secret escape hatch for beating a hasty retreat. Note: This fort requires skilled carpentry.

MATERIALS for Fort Edward

Posts

(23) 4x4 pressure-treated posts, 10 ft. long

Tree slabs

(108) 8-ft.-long slabs, 6 in. wide

Construction-grade pine or equal

180 lineal ft. of 2x6s (used to connect tree slabs to posts at three levels)

130 lineal ft. of 2x6s (additional lumber for building walk and towers)

176 lineal ft. of 2x6s (for wall walk floor decking)

Braces and railings

108 lineal ft. of 2x4 construction-grade fir

Plywood

13 sheets, 4' x 8' exterior plywood for gatehouse, tower roofs, and ramp

Additional materials required: Concrete, nails, screws, rope, hinges, dowels, and roof covering to be ordered as needed.

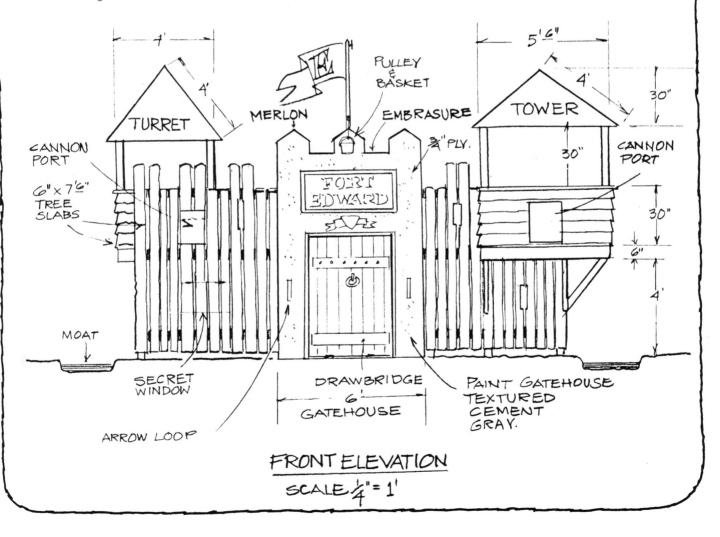

FRONT ELEVATION
SCALE ¼"= 1'

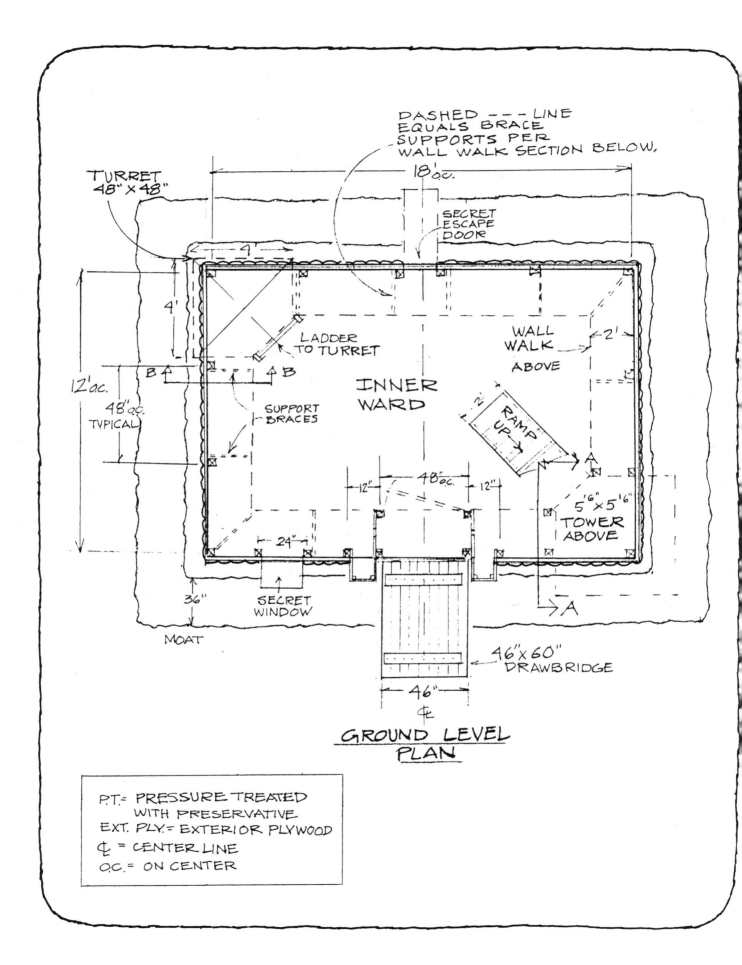

DASHED --- LINE
EQUALS BRACE
SUPPORTS PER
WALL WALK SECTION BELOW.

18' o.c.

TURRET
48" x 48"

SECRET
ESCAPE
DOOR

4'

4'

WALL
WALK
ABOVE

2'

12' o.c.

B ← →B

LADDER
TO TURRET

INNER
WARD

RAMP
UP →

2'

48" o.c.
TYPICAL

SUPPORT
BRACES

A →

A

12"   48" o.c.   12"

5'6" x 5'6"
TOWER
ABOVE

24"

36"

SECRET
WINDOW

→ A

MOAT

46" x 60"
DRAWBRIDGE

46"

¢

GROUND LEVEL
PLAN

P.T.= PRESSURE TREATED
      WITH PRESERVATIVE
EXT. PLY.= EXTERIOR PLYWOOD
¢ = CENTER LINE
O.C.= ON CENTER

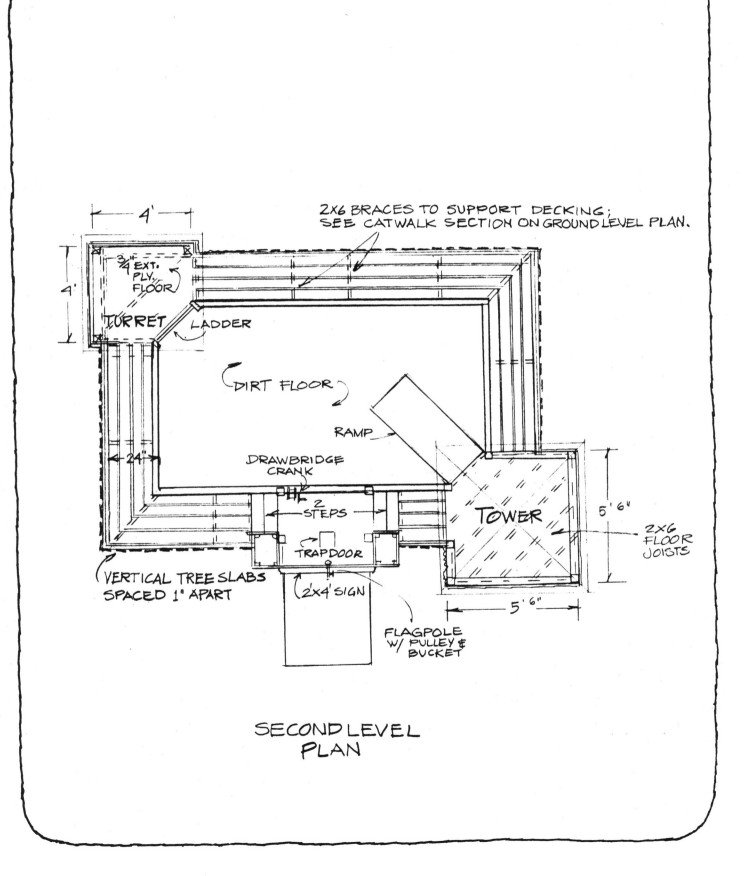

2X6 BRACES TO SUPPORT DECKING;
SEE CATWALK SECTION ON GROUND LEVEL PLAN.

4'

4'

3/4" EXT. PLY. FLOOR

TURRET

LADDER

DIRT FLOOR

RAMP

24"

DRAWBRIDGE CRANK

2 STEPS

TOWER

5'6"

2X6 FLOOR JOISTS

TRAPDOOR

2'X4' SIGN

VERTICAL TREE SLABS
SPACED 1" APART

FLAGPOLE
W/ PULLEY &
BUCKET

5'6"

SECOND LEVEL
PLAN

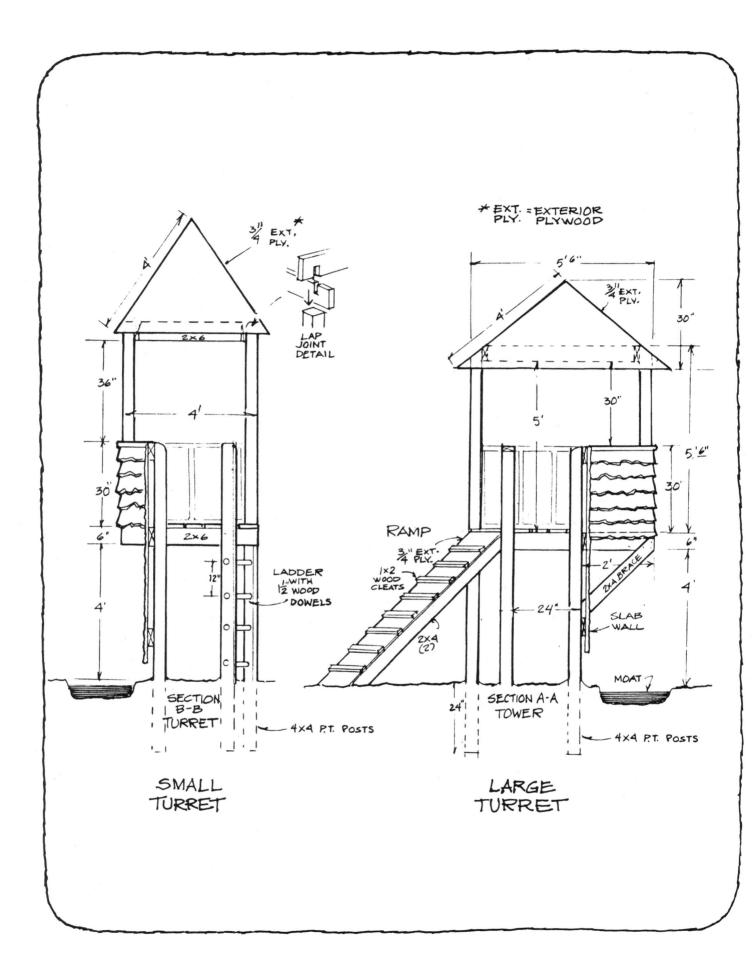

LAP
JOINT
DETAIL

*EXT. = EXTERIOR
PLY.   PLYWOOD

3/4" EXT. PLY.

2×6

36"

4'

30"

6"

12"

4'

LADDER
WITH 1/2" WOOD
DOWELS

2×6

SECTION
B-B
TURRET

4×4 P.T. POSTS

SMALL
TURRET

5'6"

4'

3/4" EXT. PLY.

30"

5'

30"

5'6"

30"

6"

4'

RAMP

3/4" EXT. PLY.

1×2 WOOD CLEATS

2×4 (2)

24"

2×4 BRACE

2'

SLAB WALL

MOAT

SECTION A-A
TOWER

24"

4×4 P.T. POSTS

LARGE
TURRET

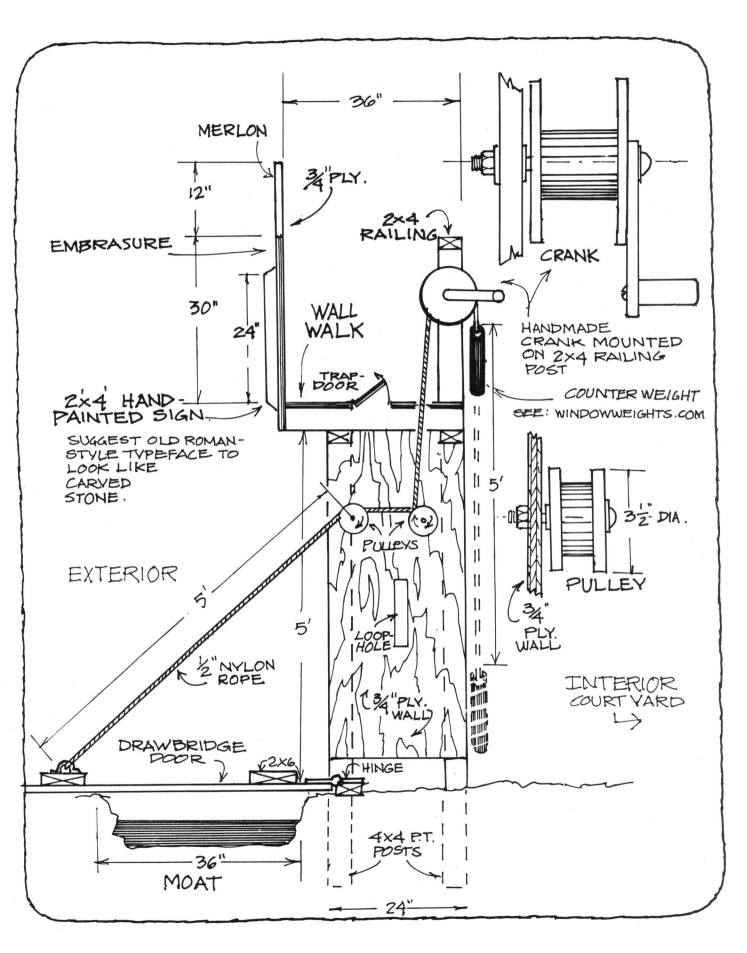

MERLON

3/4" PLY.

36"

2x4 RAILING

CRANK

12"

EMBRASURE

30"

24"

WALL WALK

HANDMADE CRANK MOUNTED ON 2x4 RAILING POST

COUNTER WEIGHT
SEE: WINDOWWEIGHTS.COM

TRAP-DOOR

2'x4' HAND-PAINTED SIGN.

SUGGEST OLD ROMAN-STYLE TYPEFACE TO LOOK LIKE CARVED STONE.

5'

PULLEYS

3 1/2" DIA.

PULLEY

EXTERIOR

5'

5'

LOOP-HOLE

3/4" PLY. WALL

INTERIOR COURT YARD

1/2" NYLON ROPE

3/4" PLY. WALL

DRAWBRIDGE DOOR

2x6

HINGE

MOAT

4x4 P.T. POSTS

36"

24"

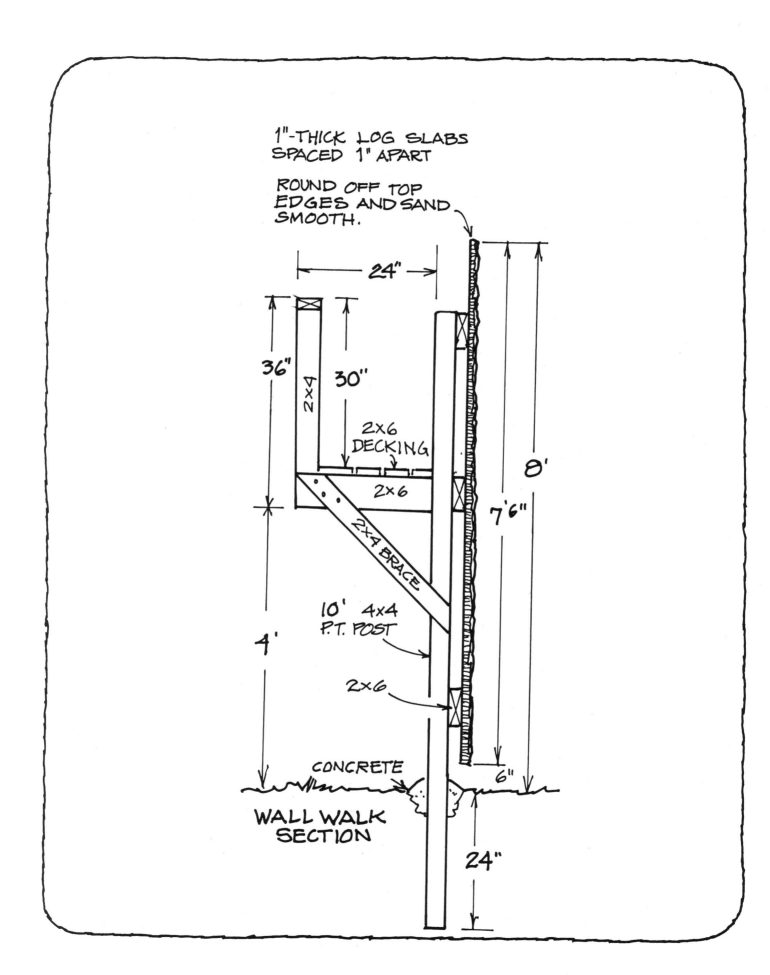

1"-THICK LOG SLABS
SPACED 1" APART

ROUND OFF TOP
EDGES AND SAND
SMOOTH.

24"

36"

30"

2×4

2×6
DECKING

2×6

2×4 BRACE

8'

7'6"

10' 4×4
P.T. POST

4'

2×6

CONCRETE

6"

WALL WALK
SECTION

24"

NOTE: RIP (SAW) BOTH SIDES OF EACH SLAB SQUARE SO THAT EACH SLAB IS 6" WIDE.

6"

TREE SLAB SECTION

4X4 P.T. POST

2X6

POST HOLE DIGGER

6"

PROP FOR HOLDING BOARDS UP 6" OFF THE GROUND WHILE NAILING

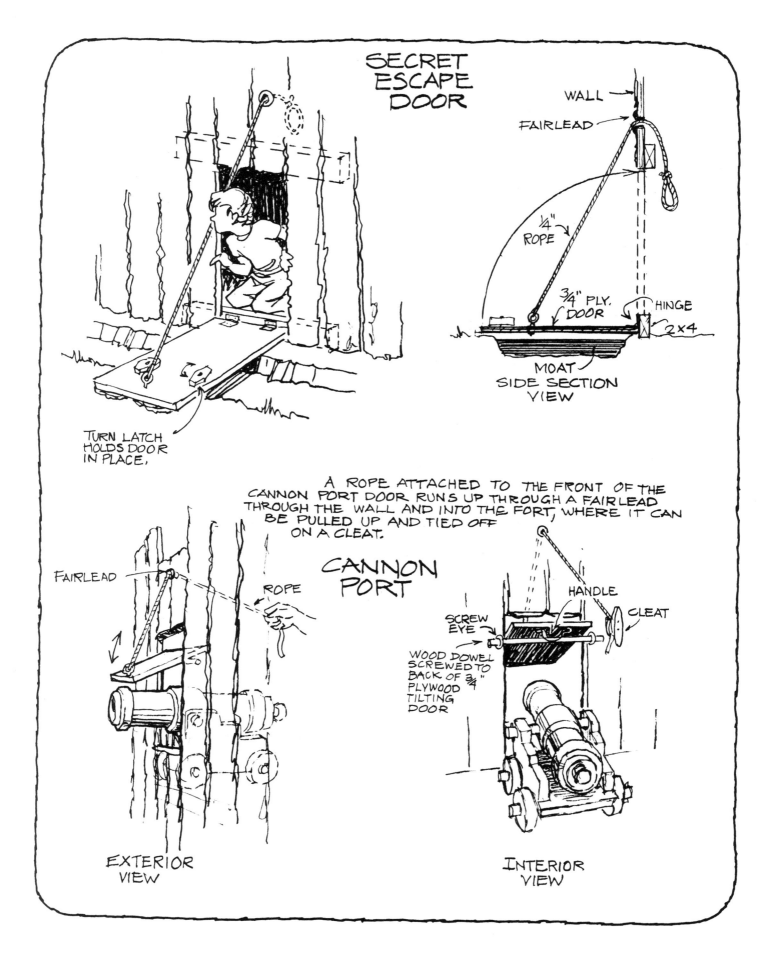

SECRET ESCAPE DOOR

WALL

FAIRLEAD

¼" ROPE

¾" PLY. DOOR

HINGE

2×4

MOAT

SIDE SECTION VIEW

TURN LATCH HOLDS DOOR IN PLACE.

A ROPE ATTACHED TO THE FRONT OF THE CANNON PORT DOOR RUNS UP THROUGH A FAIRLEAD THROUGH THE WALL AND INTO THE FORT, WHERE IT CAN BE PULLED UP AND TIED OFF ON A CLEAT.

CANNON PORT

FAIRLEAD

ROPE

HANDLE

CLEAT

SCREW EYE

WOOD DOWEL SCREWED TO BACK OF ¾" PLYWOOD TILTING DOOR

EXTERIOR VIEW

INTERIOR VIEW

70

Pirate Ship

THIS PIRATE SHIP IS SUSPENDED BETWEEN TWO TREES (MIN. 16 FEET APART) AND IS ACCESSED BY TWO FLEXIBLE BOARDING RAMPS. IN THE CENTER IS A MAST WITH RUNGS TO CLIMB UP FOR USE AS A LOOKOUT. THE BOTTOM OF THE MAST IS USED AS A FIREPOLE FOR QUICK EXITS. THE BOARDING RAMPS ARE SECURED TO THE GROUND TO PREVENT THE PIRATE SHIP FROM FLIPPING OVER, ALLOWING THE SHIP TO SWAY SLIGHTLY IN THE WIND, WHICH GIVES THE IMPRESSION OF FLOATING ON THE SEA.

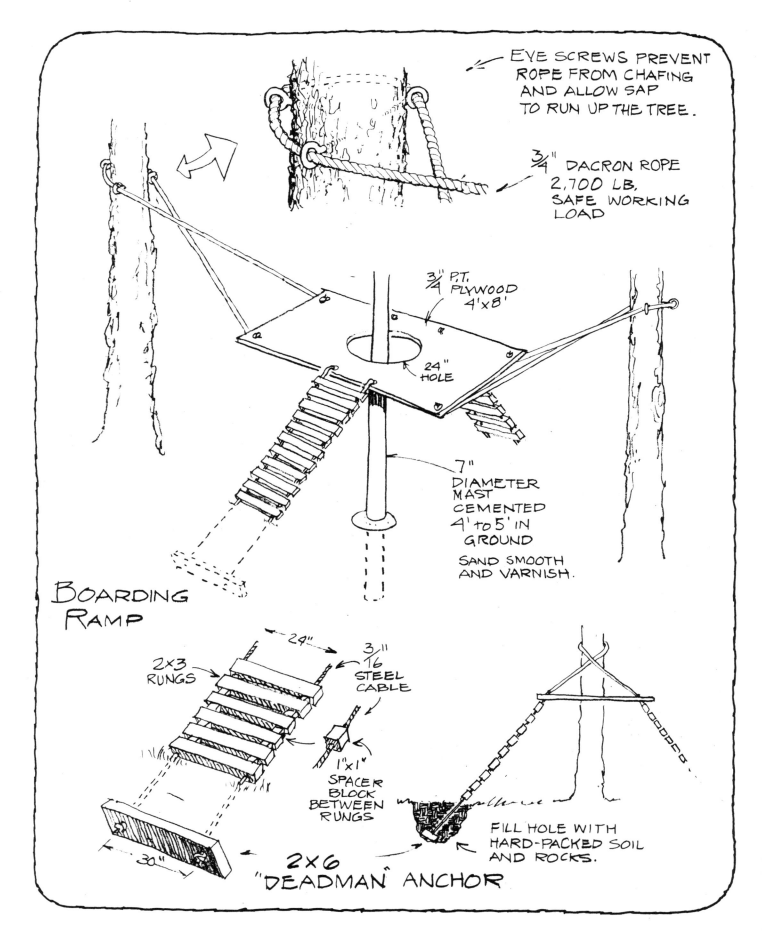

EYE SCREWS PREVENT ROPE FROM CHAFING AND ALLOW SAP TO RUN UP THE TREE.

¾" DACRON ROPE 2,700 LB, SAFE WORKING LOAD

¾" P.T. PLYWOOD 4'x8'

24" HOLE

7" DIAMETER MAST CEMENTED 4' to 5' IN GROUND

SAND SMOOTH AND VARNISH.

BOARDING RAMP

24"

2x3 RUNGS

3/16" STEEL CABLE

1"x1" SPACER BLOCK BETWEEN RUNGS

30"

2x6 "DEADMAN" ANCHOR

FILL HOLE WITH HARD-PACKED SOIL AND ROCKS.

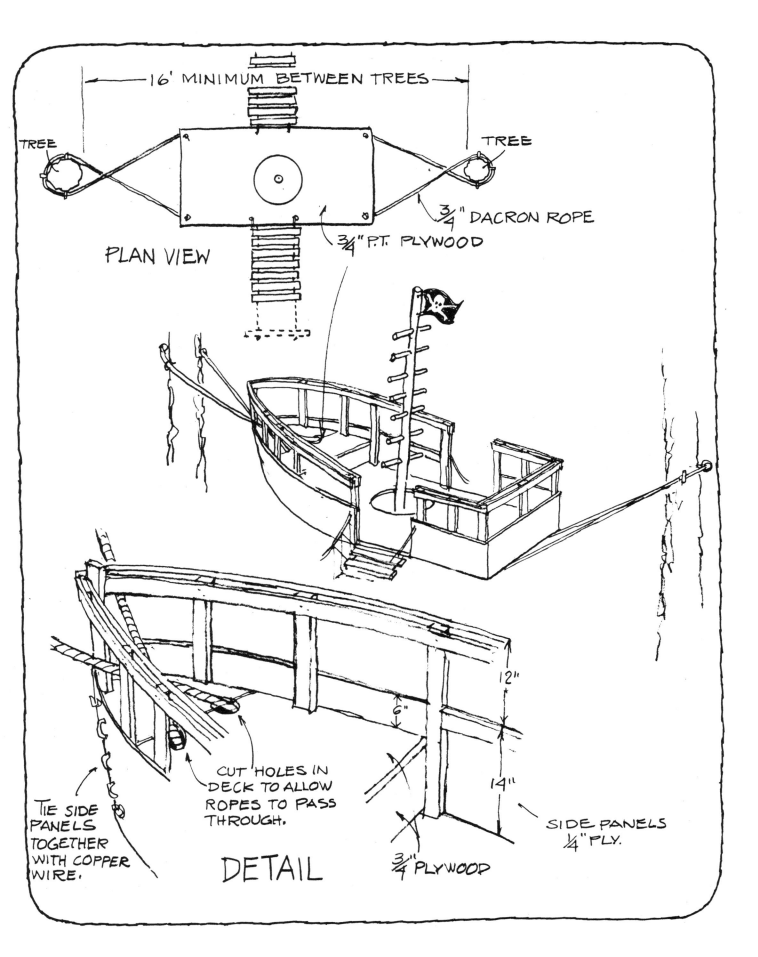

16' MINIMUM BETWEEN TREES

TREE

TREE

PLAN VIEW

¾" DACRON ROPE

¾" P.T. PLYWOOD

CUT HOLES IN DECK TO ALLOW ROPES TO PASS THROUGH.

TIE SIDE PANELS TOGETHER WITH COPPER WIRE.

DETAIL

12"

6"

14"

¾" PLYWOOD

SIDE PANELS ¼" PLY.

TANK

THIS MOBILE FORTRESS (TANK) WILL REALLY IMPRESS YOUR
NEIGHBORS. YOU CAN MOVE IT WITHOUT BEING SEEN
BY OPENING A TRAPDOOR IN THE BOTTOM AND PUSHING
THE TANK FROM THE INSIDE. IT FEATURES A SWIVEL
TURRET WITH A CANNON THAT CAN BE FITTED WITH A WATER
GUN TO SURPRISE THE "ENEMY."

THIS TANK IS MADE OUT OF PLYWOOD, RECYCLED BICYCLE
WHEELS, AND SOME PLUMBING PIPE. ACCESS IS THROUGH
A HATCH IN THE TOP TURRET OR THROUGH A TRAPDOOR
IN THE BACK. PAINT IT OLIVE DRAB.

74

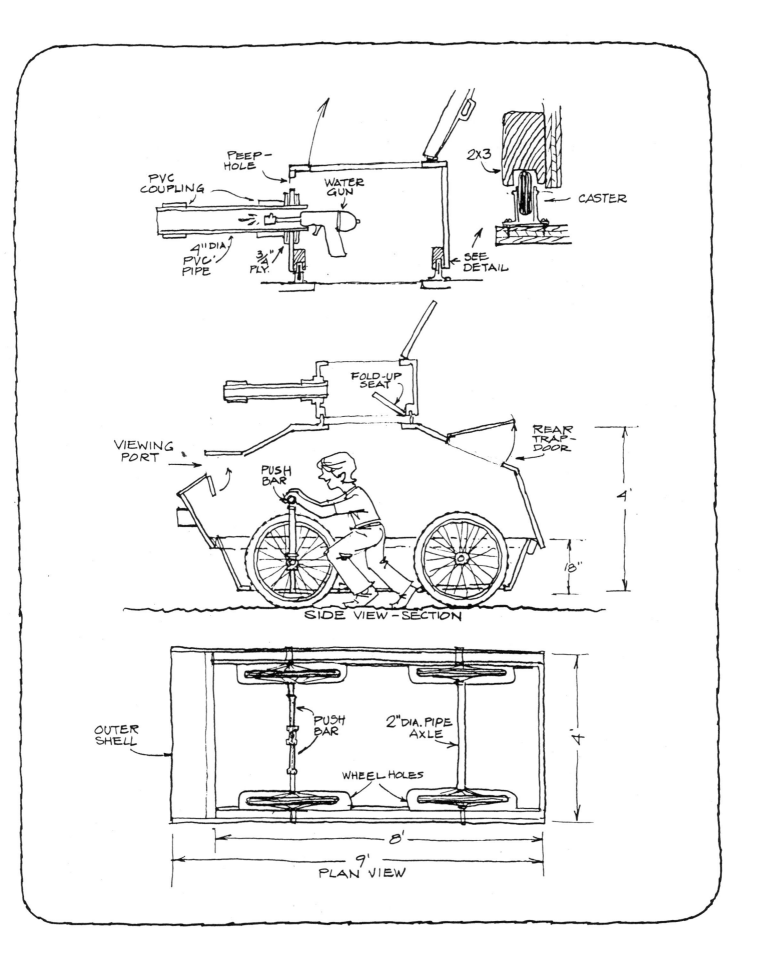

PEEP-
HOLE

PVC
COUPLING

2x3

WATER
GUN

CASTER

4" DIA.
PVC
PIPE

3/4"
PLY.

SEE
DETAIL

FOLD-UP
SEAT

REAR
TRAP-
DOOR

VIEWING
PORT

PUSH
BAR

4'

18"

SIDE VIEW – SECTION

OUTER
SHELL

PUSH
BAR

2" DIA. PIPE
AXLE

4'

WHEEL HOLES

8'

9'

PLAN VIEW

75

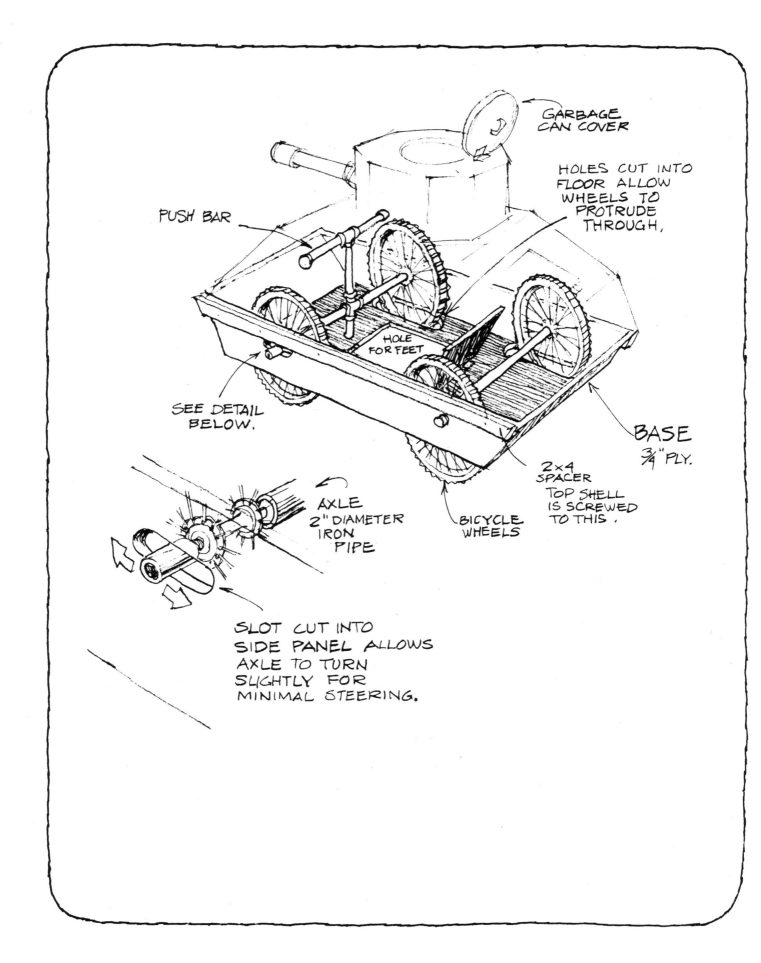

GARBAGE
CAN COVER

HOLES CUT INTO
FLOOR ALLOW
WHEELS TO
PROTRUDE
THROUGH.

PUSH BAR

HOLE
FOR FEET

SEE DETAIL
BELOW.

BASE
¾" PLY.

2×4
SPACER
TOP SHELL
IS SCREWED
TO THIS.

BICYCLE
WHEELS

AXLE
2" DIAMETER
IRON
PIPE

SLOT CUT INTO
SIDE PANEL ALLOWS
AXLE TO TURN
SLIGHTLY FOR
MINIMAL STEERING.

FORT TOYS

It may become necessary to protect yourself from potential "invaders". An arsenal of fort toys can be made with materials found around the house; however, they <u>must</u> be safe.

A safe fort toy fires only soft, harmless ammunition such as pillows, balloons, wiffle balls, foam balls, tennis balls, ping-pong balls, snowballs, and soap bubbles, to name a few. In the summer you can use water guns or make water bombs out of balloons. Although these things are considered safe, there is one rule that <u>must</u> be obeyed by all. That is:

NEVER AIM OR FIRE AT SOMEONE'S HEAD

Make it understood that any kid who disobeys this rule will be immediately sent home by the other kids for the rest of the day.

In addition it should also be understood that:

1. No dangerous guns such as BB guns are allowed
2. No matches
3. No firecrackers
4. No tying up another person with rope
5. No pushing or shoving or calling bad names
6. No ice in snowballs

Water Balloon Launcher

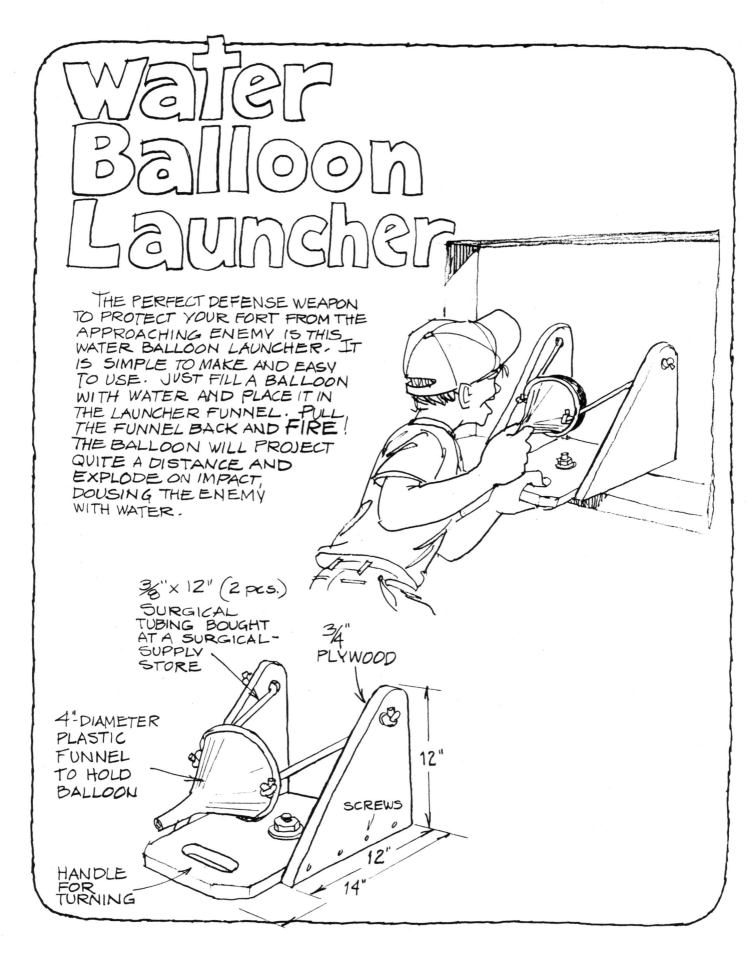

THE PERFECT DEFENSE WEAPON TO PROTECT YOUR FORT FROM THE APPROACHING ENEMY IS THIS WATER BALLOON LAUNCHER. IT IS SIMPLE TO MAKE AND EASY TO USE. JUST FILL A BALLOON WITH WATER AND PLACE IT IN THE LAUNCHER FUNNEL. PULL THE FUNNEL BACK AND FIRE! THE BALLOON WILL PROJECT QUITE A DISTANCE AND EXPLODE ON IMPACT, DOUSING THE ENEMY WITH WATER.

3/8" × 12" (2 pcs.) SURGICAL TUBING BOUGHT AT A SURGICAL-SUPPLY STORE

3/4" PLYWOOD

4"-DIAMETER PLASTIC FUNNEL TO HOLD BALLOON

12"

SCREWS

12"

14"

HANDLE FOR TURNING

ALL YOU NEED IS A PIECE OF
14" x 12" x ¾" PLYWOOD AND...   4"x 2"
HANDLE
HOLE

...A 12"x12" PIECE OF PLYWOOD
CUT DIAGONALLY IN HALF.

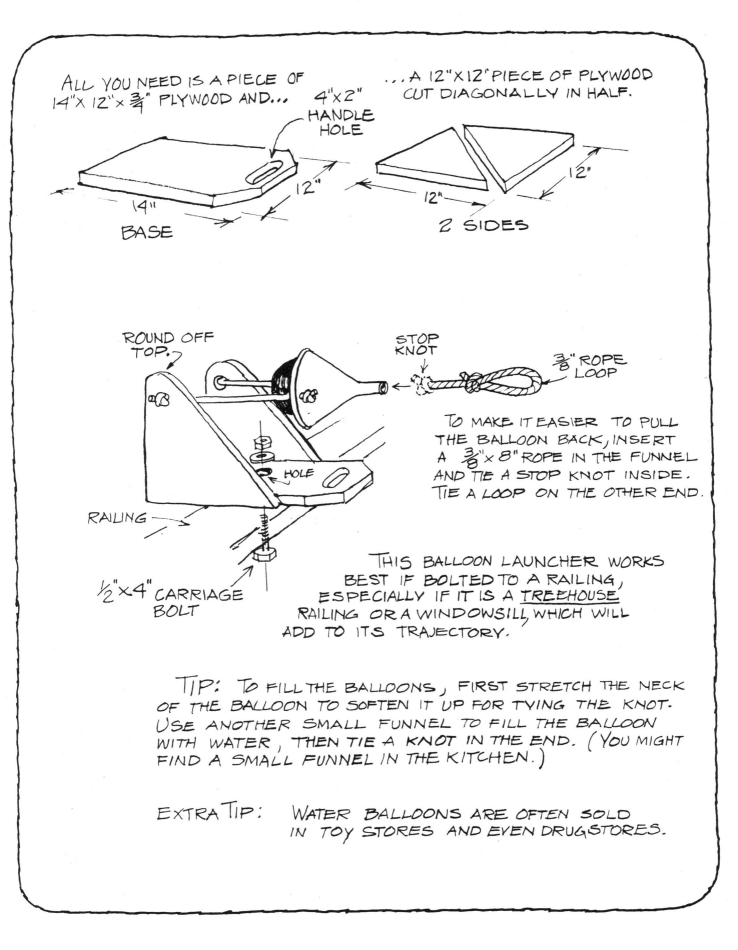

12"

14"

BASE

12"

12"

2 SIDES

ROUND OFF
TOP.

STOP
KNOT

⅜" ROPE
LOOP

RAILING

HOLE

½"x4" CARRIAGE
BOLT

TO MAKE IT EASIER TO PULL
THE BALLOON BACK, INSERT
A ⅜"x 8" ROPE IN THE FUNNEL
AND TIE A STOP KNOT INSIDE.
TIE A LOOP ON THE OTHER END.

THIS BALLOON LAUNCHER WORKS
BEST IF BOLTED TO A RAILING,
ESPECIALLY IF IT IS A <u>TREEHOUSE</u>
RAILING OR A WINDOWSILL, WHICH WILL
ADD TO ITS TRAJECTORY.

TIP: TO FILL THE BALLOONS, FIRST STRETCH THE NECK
OF THE BALLOON TO SOFTEN IT UP FOR TYING THE KNOT.
USE ANOTHER SMALL FUNNEL TO FILL THE BALLOON
WITH WATER, THEN TIE A KNOT IN THE END. (YOU MIGHT
FIND A SMALL FUNNEL IN THE KITCHEN.)

EXTRA TIP: WATER BALLOONS ARE OFTEN SOLD
IN TOY STORES AND EVEN DRUGSTORES.

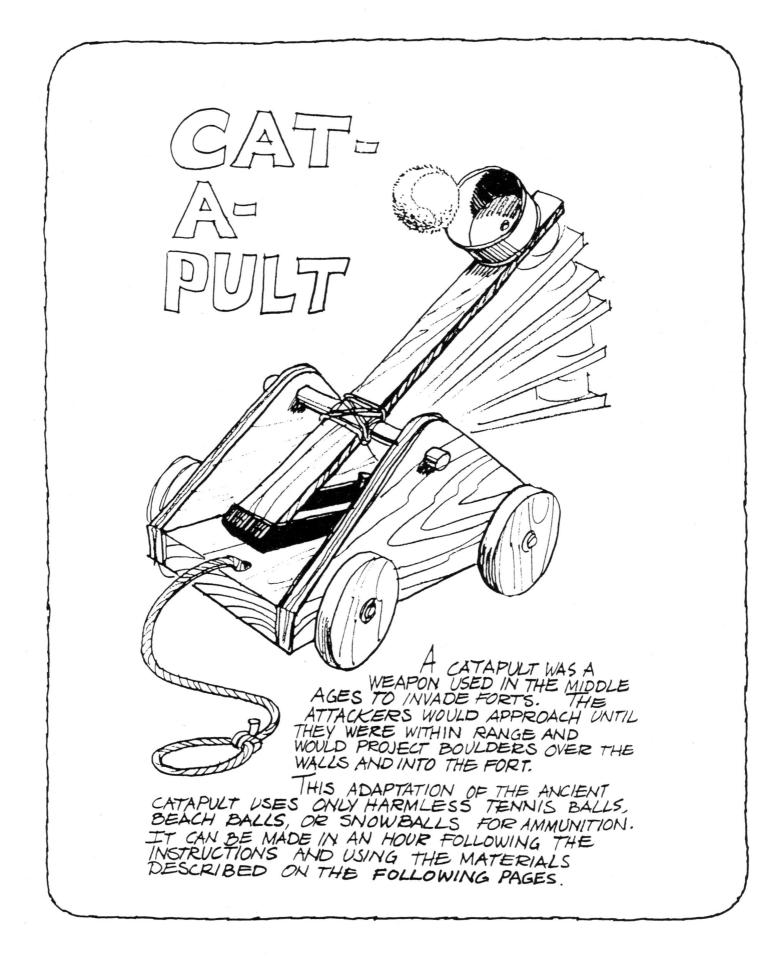

CAT- A- PULT

A CATAPULT WAS A WEAPON USED IN THE MIDDLE AGES TO INVADE FORTS. THE ATTACKERS WOULD APPROACH UNTIL THEY WERE WITHIN RANGE AND WOULD PROJECT BOULDERS OVER THE WALLS AND INTO THE FORT.

THIS ADAPTATION OF THE ANCIENT CATAPULT USES ONLY HARMLESS TENNIS BALLS, BEACH BALLS, OR SNOWBALLS FOR AMMUNITION. IT CAN BE MADE IN AN HOUR FOLLOWING THE INSTRUCTIONS AND USING THE MATERIALS DESCRIBED ON THE FOLLOWING PAGES.

MATERIALS:

ONE	3/4" THICK PLYWOOD	12" x 12"	SIDES
ONE	1/2" THICK BOARD	24" LONG x 2"	ARM
ONE	2x8 BOARD	16" LONG	BASE
ONE	3/4" DOWEL	10" LONG	PIVOT
THREE	3/4" DOWELS	2" LONG	PEGS
TWO	HEAVY STRINGS	1 YARD LONG	
ONE	1" RUBBER BAND 8" LONG (CUT FROM OLD INNER TUBE)		
EIGHT	1 1/2" FINISHING NAILS		

CUT A PIECE OF 3/4" X 12" X 12"
PLYWOOD ACROSS THE DIAGONAL
TO FORM TWO TRIANGLES.

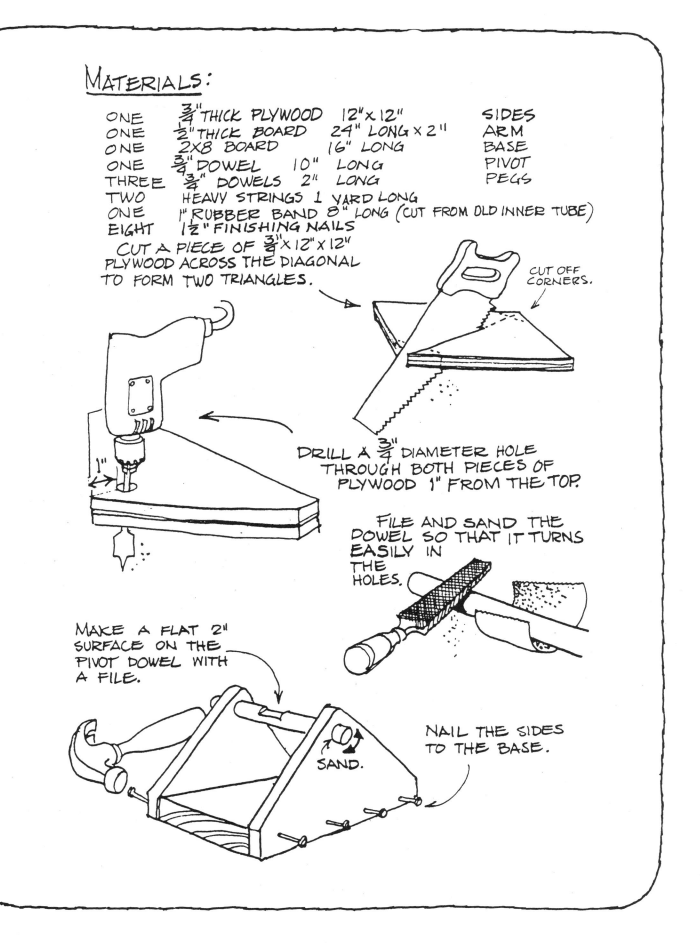

CUT OFF CORNERS.

DRILL A 3/4" DIAMETER HOLE
THROUGH BOTH PIECES OF
PLYWOOD 1" FROM THE TOP.

FILE AND SAND THE DOWEL SO THAT IT TURNS EASILY IN THE HOLES.

MAKE A FLAT 2"
SURFACE ON THE
PIVOT DOWEL WITH
A FILE.

SAND.

NAIL THE SIDES
TO THE BASE.

81

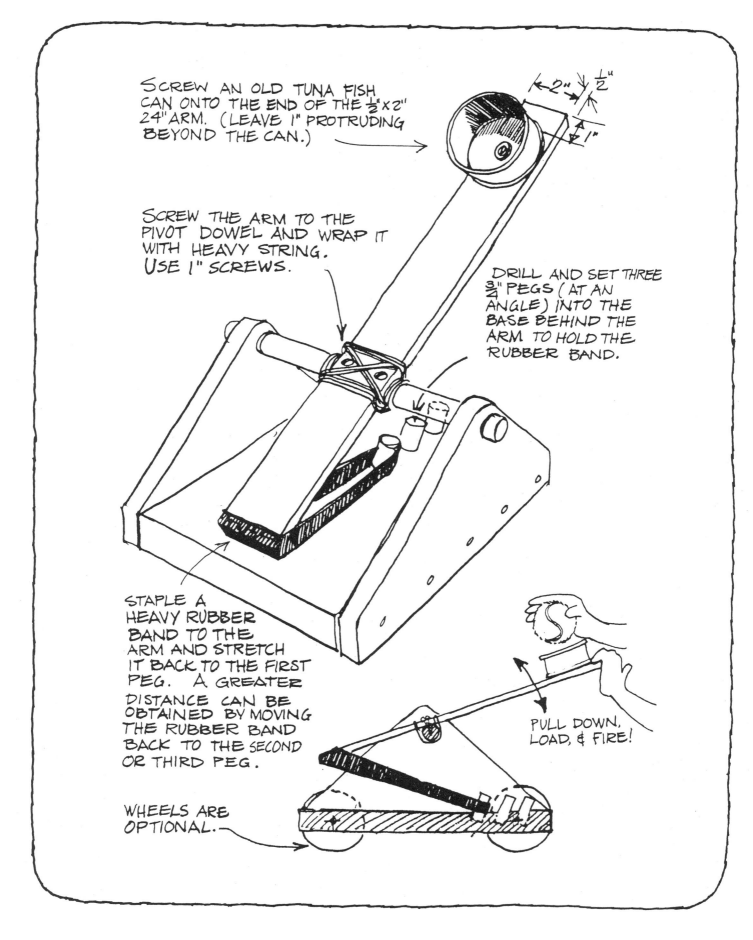

SCREW AN OLD TUNA FISH CAN ONTO THE END OF THE ½"×2" 24" ARM. (LEAVE 1" PROTRUDING BEYOND THE CAN.)

SCREW THE ARM TO THE PIVOT DOWEL AND WRAP IT WITH HEAVY STRING. USE 1" SCREWS.

DRILL AND SET THREE ¾" PEGS (AT AN ANGLE) INTO THE BASE BEHIND THE ARM TO HOLD THE RUBBER BAND.

STAPLE A HEAVY RUBBER BAND TO THE ARM AND STRETCH IT BACK TO THE FIRST PEG. A GREATER DISTANCE CAN BE OBTAINED BY MOVING THE RUBBER BAND BACK TO THE SECOND OR THIRD PEG.

WHEELS ARE OPTIONAL.

PULL DOWN, LOAD, & FIRE!

TrebucheT

(TRAY-boo-SHAY)

THE TREBUCHET WAS USED IN ANCIENT TIMES TO LAY SIEGE TO A FORTRESS BY BREACHING THE WALLS. LIKE A CATAPULT, IT USES A WEIGHT TO SPRING THE ARM FORWARD, BUT HAS THE ADVANTAGE OF A SLING TO INCREASE THE THROWING DISTANCE CONSIDERABLY.

THIS TREBUCHET CAN BE BUILT USING LEFTOVER LUMBER AND TAKES LESS THAN A DAY TO MAKE. IT MUST ONLY BE USED TO HURL HARMLESS WATER BALLOONS.

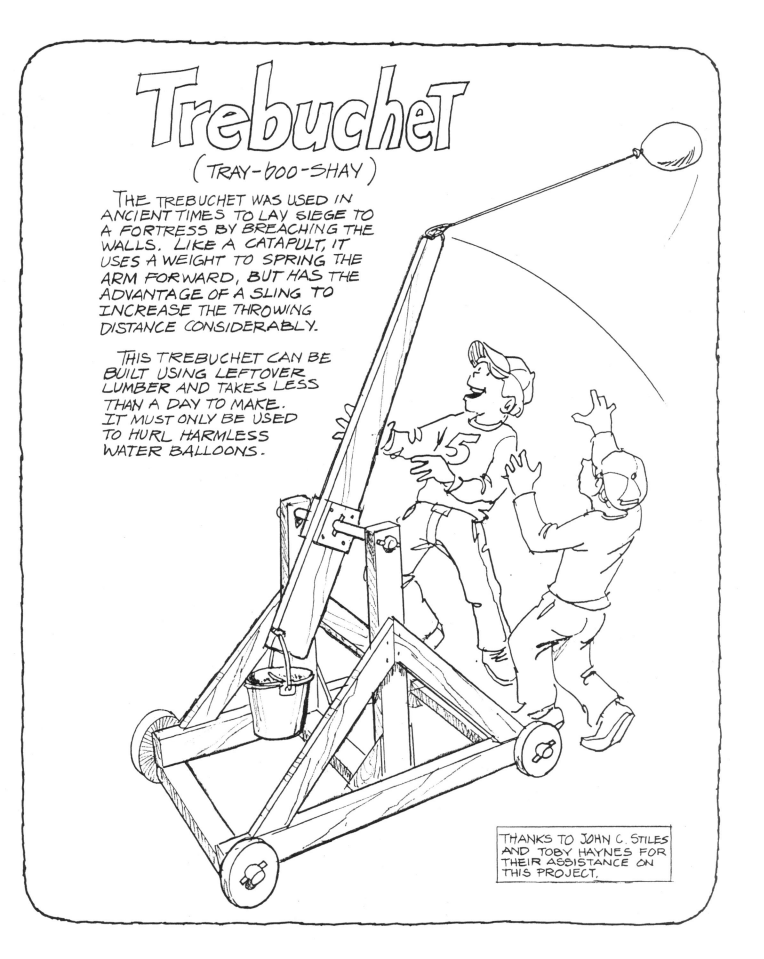

THANKS TO JOHN C. STILES AND TOBY HAYNES FOR THEIR ASSISTANCE ON THIS PROJECT.

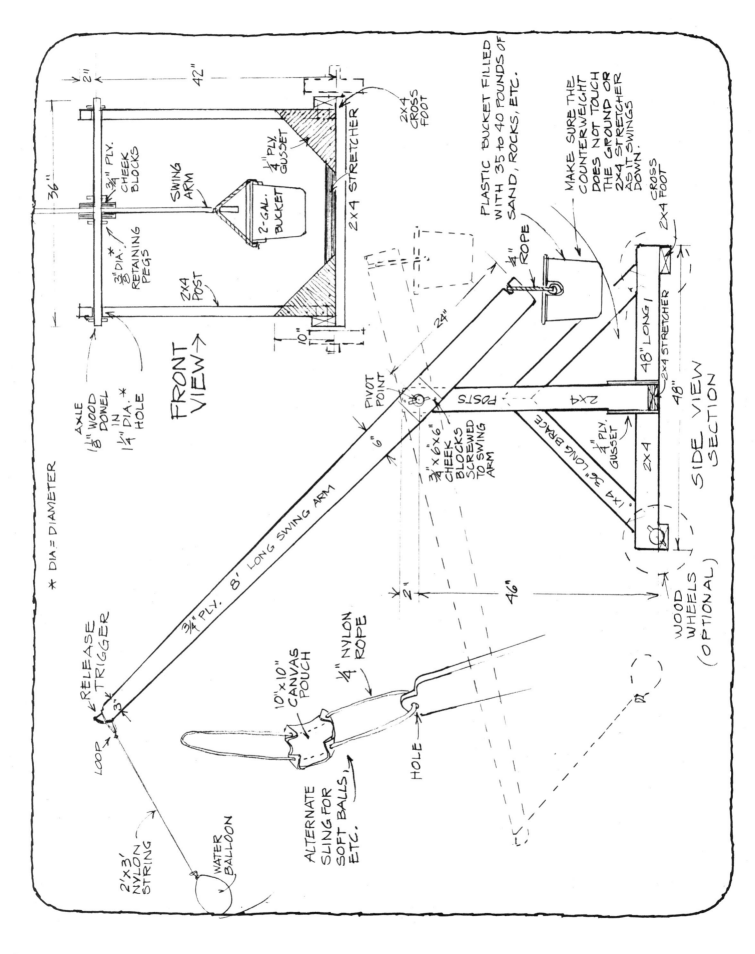

* DIA = DIAMETER

2"

42"

36"

¾" PLY.
CHEEK
BLOCKS

SWING ARM

2-GAL.
BUCKET

¼" PLY.
GUSSET

2x4
CROSS
FOOT

2x4 STRETCHER

⅜" DIA. *
RETAINING
PEGS

2x4
POST

10"

AXLE
1⅛" WOOD
DOWEL
IN
1¼" DIA. *
HOLE

FRONT VIEW→

PLASTIC BUCKET FILLED
WITH 35 to 40 POUNDS OF
SAND, ROCKS, ETC.

MAKE SURE THE
COUNTERWEIGHT
DOES NOT TOUCH
THE GROUND OR
2x4 STRETCHER
AS IT SWINGS
DOWN.

¼" ROPE

24"

PIVOT
POINT

6"

3"x6x6"
CHEEK BLOCKS
SCREWED TO
SWING ARM

2x4 POSTS

2x4

¼" PLY.
GUSSET

36" LONG BRACE

2x4

48" LONG

2x4 STRETCHER

48"

2x4 FOOT

CROSS

SIDE VIEW
SECTION

WOOD
WHEELS
(OPTIONAL)

2"

46"

¾" PLY. 8' LONG SWING ARM

RELEASE
TRIGGER

3"

LOOP

2'x3'
NYLON
STRING

WATER
BALLOON

10"x10"
CANVAS
POUCH

¼" NYLON
ROPE

HOLE

ALTERNATE
SLING FOR
SOFT BALLS,
ETC.

TO ACHIEVE A GREATER DISTANCE, YOU CAN EXPERIMENT BY ADDING A LONGER SLING, INCREASING THE HEIGHT OF THE PIVOT POINT, INCREASING THE WEIGHT OF THE COUNTERWEIGHT, OR INCREASING THE LENGTH OF THE ARM. TIP: USE A PARTIALLY FILLED 1-QUART PLASTIC MILK BOTTLE TO EXPERIMENT WITH, BUT MAKE SURE NO ONE IS IN THE WAY.

THE BEST AMMUNITION IS A BALLOON FILLED WITH WATER.

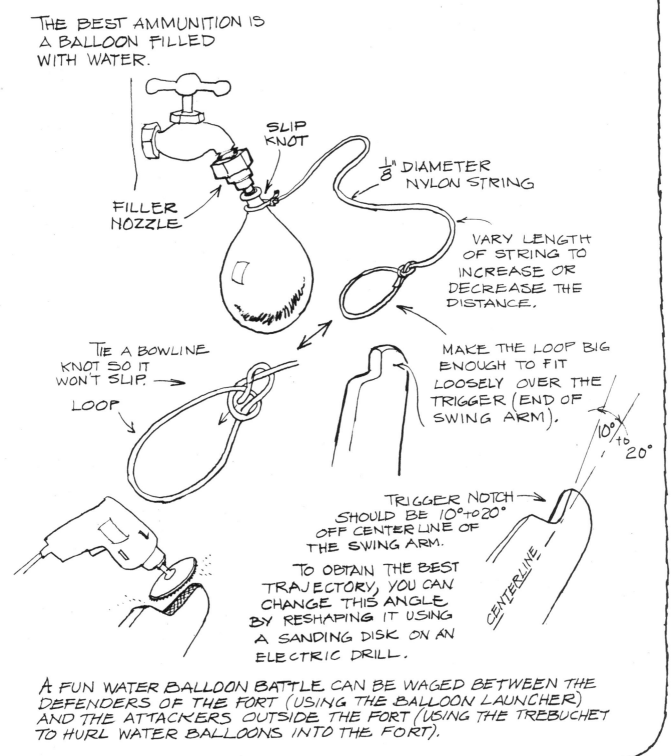

SLIP KNOT

FILLER NOZZLE

$\frac{1}{8}$" DIAMETER NYLON STRING

VARY LENGTH OF STRING TO INCREASE OR DECREASE THE DISTANCE.

TIE A BOWLINE KNOT SO IT WON'T SLIP. →

LOOP

MAKE THE LOOP BIG ENOUGH TO FIT LOOSELY OVER THE TRIGGER (END OF SWING ARM).

10° to 20°

TRIGGER NOTCH →

TRIGGER NOTCH SHOULD BE 10° to 20° OFF CENTER LINE OF THE SWING ARM.

TO OBTAIN THE BEST TRAJECTORY, YOU CAN CHANGE THIS ANGLE BY RESHAPING IT USING A SANDING DISK ON AN ELECTRIC DRILL.

CENTERLINE

A FUN WATER BALLOON BATTLE CAN BE WAGED BETWEEN THE DEFENDERS OF THE FORT (USING THE BALLOON LAUNCHER) AND THE ATTACKERS OUTSIDE THE FORT (USING THE TREBUCHET TO HURL WATER BALLOONS INTO THE FORT).

Ghost Ship Periscope

To make a periscope more interesting and more of a challenge, you might try this idea:

Build the periscope out of $\frac{3}{8}$" plywood and two mirrors (even plastic ones will do).

Take a photo of an old pirate ship (found on the internet) to a photo store and ask them to make a 3" x 5" negative of the ship.

Mount the negative between two pieces of glass or plastic, and tape the edges so that no moisture can seep through the pieces and ruin the negative.

Place the encased negative in a $\frac{1}{8}$" slot under the top window and secure it with removable set screws.

The best way to see the ghost ship is to turn the periscope toward the light.

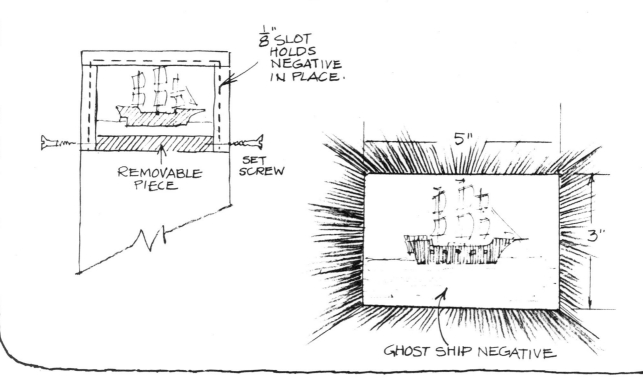

$\frac{1}{8}$" SLOT HOLDS NEGATIVE IN PLACE.

REMOVABLE PIECE

SET SCREW

5"

3"

GHOST SHIP NEGATIVE

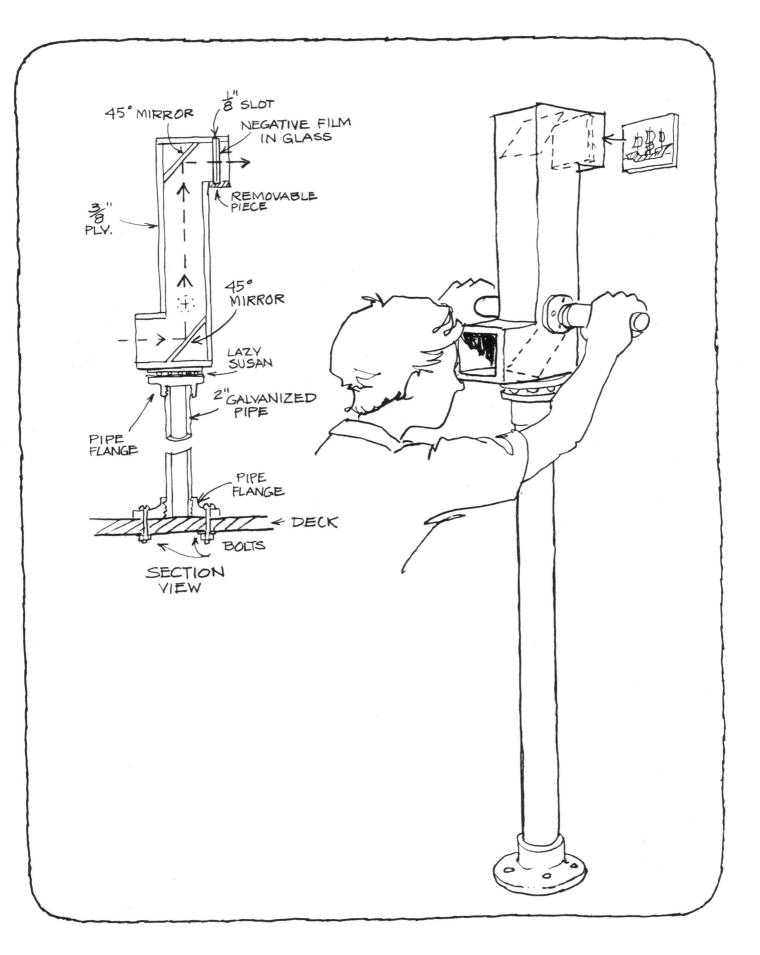

45° MIRROR

$\frac{1}{8}$" SLOT

NEGATIVE FILM IN GLASS

$\frac{3}{8}$" PLY.

REMOVABLE PIECE

45° MIRROR

LAZY SUSAN

2" GALVANIZED PIPE

PIPE FLANGE

PIPE FLANGE

DECK

BOLTS

SECTION VIEW

CANNON

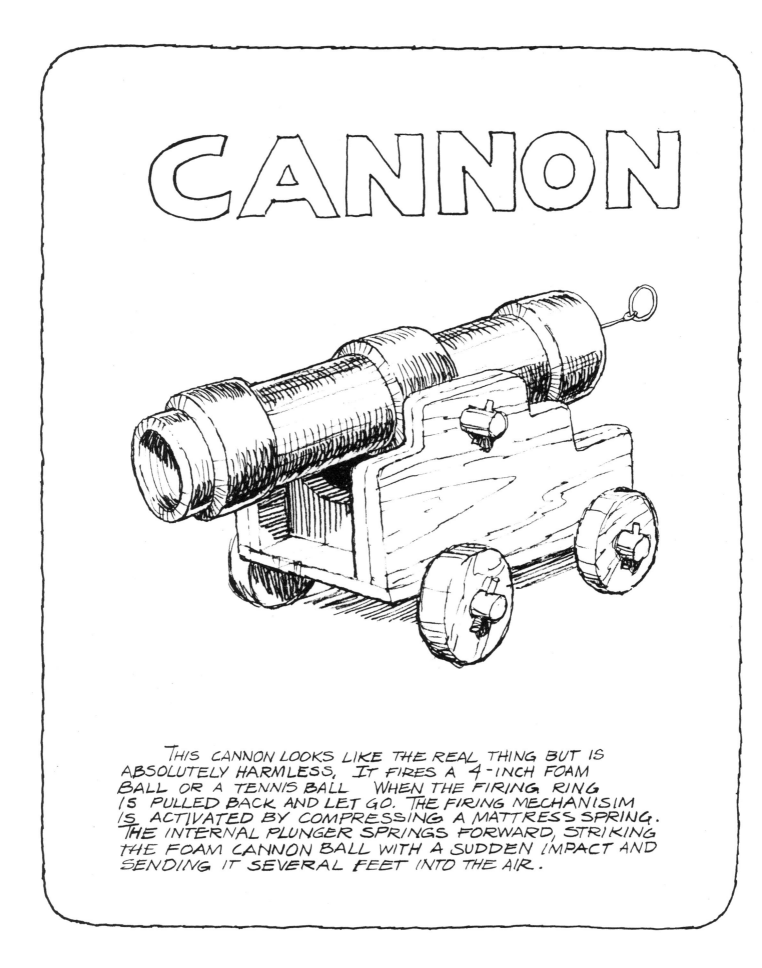

THIS CANNON LOOKS LIKE THE REAL THING BUT IS ABSOLUTELY HARMLESS. IT FIRES A 4-INCH FOAM BALL OR A TENNIS BALL WHEN THE FIRING RING IS PULLED BACK AND LET GO. THE FIRING MECHANISIM IS ACTIVATED BY COMPRESSING A MATTRESS SPRING. THE INTERNAL PLUNGER SPRINGS FORWARD, STRIKING THE FOAM CANNON BALL WITH A SUDDEN IMPACT AND SENDING IT SEVERAL FEET INTO THE AIR.

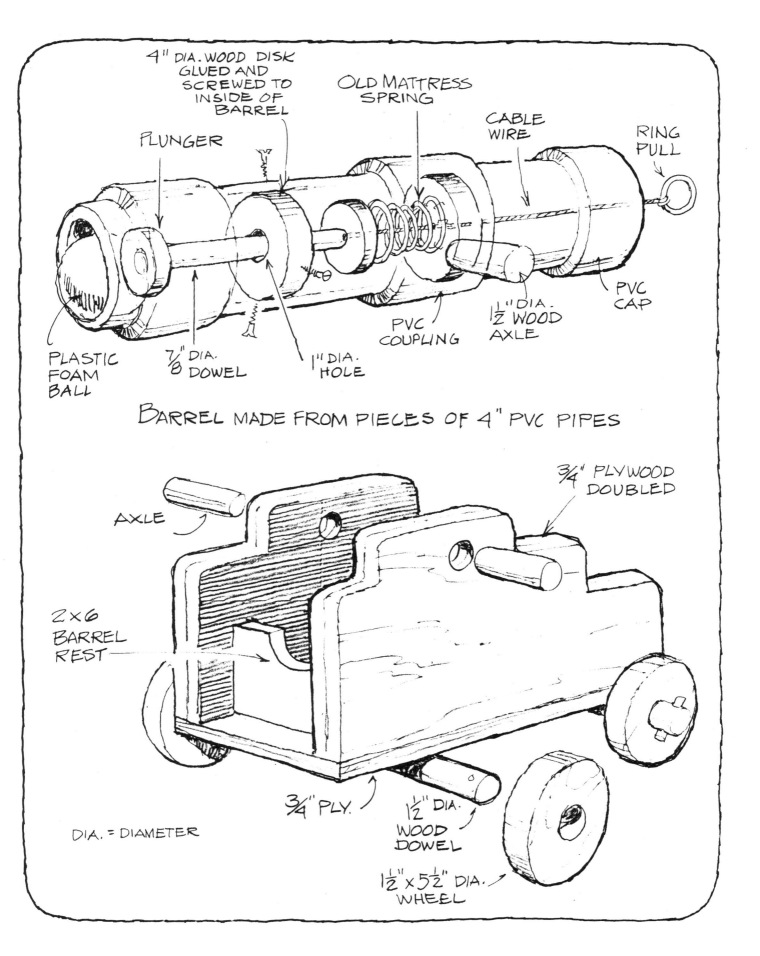

4" DIA. WOOD DISK GLUED AND SCREWED TO INSIDE OF BARREL

OLD MATTRESS SPRING

CABLE WIRE

RING PULL

PLUNGER

PVC CAP

PLASTIC FOAM BALL

$\frac{7}{8}$" DIA. DOWEL

1" DIA. HOLE

PVC COUPLING

$1\frac{1}{2}$" DIA. WOOD AXLE

BARREL MADE FROM PIECES OF 4" PVC PIPES

AXLE

$\frac{3}{4}$" PLYWOOD DOUBLED

2×6 BARREL REST

$\frac{3}{4}$" PLY.

$1\frac{1}{2}$" DIA. WOOD DOWEL

DIA. = DIAMETER

$1\frac{1}{2}$" × $5\frac{1}{2}$" DIA. WHEEL

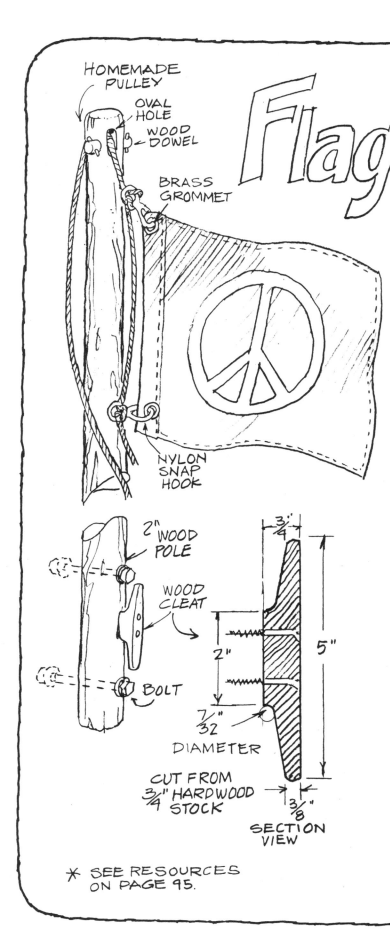

Flags

HOMEMADE PULLEY

OVAL HOLE

WOOD DOWEL

BRASS GROMMET

NYLON SNAP HOOK

2" WOOD POLE

WOOD CLEAT

BOLT

2"

5"

3/4"

7/32" DIAMETER

3/8"

SECTION VIEW

CUT FROM 3/4" HARDWOOD STOCK

✱ SEE RESOURCES ON PAGE 95.

EVERY FORT SHOULD HAVE A FLAG TO IDENTIFY IT. BESIDES, FLAGS ARE A LOT OF FUN TO HOIST UP AND DOWN. YOU CAN MAKE YOUR OWN FLAGS FROM OLD BEDSHEETS BUT NYLON CLOTH WILL LAST LONGER.

FLAGS SHOULD BE ATTACHED BY BRASS GROMMETS,✱ WHICH ARE EASY TO INSTALL. THE OUTSIDE EDGE SHOULD BE HEMMED WITH NEEDLE AND THREAD SO THAT IT DOES NOT BECOME UNRAVELED.

FLAGPOLES CAN BE EITHER ROUND OR SQUARE (2×2) AND SHOULD BE ATTACHED TO THE FORT WITH TWO BOLTS. THE REASON FOR THIS IS BECAUSE IF THE FLAG EVER GOT STUCK AT THE TOP, YOU COULD UNDO ONE BOLT, TIP THE FLAGPOLE DOWN TO THE GROUND, AND FIX IT.

USE 1/4" POLYESTER ROPE FOR THE HALYARD ROPE AND ATTACH IT TO THE FLAG USING NYLON SNAP HOOKS.✱

THE FLAGPOLE SHOULD HAVE A CLEAT NEAR THE BOTTOM TO KEEP THE HALYARD FROM BLOWING AROUND.

YOU CAN MAKE YOUR OWN PULLEY AT THE TOP OF THE FLAGPOLE BY INSTALLING A LOOSE WOODEN DOWEL AS SHOWN ABOVE. DRILL A LARGE OVAL HOLE CROSS-WISE FOR THE ROPE TO SLIDE THROUGH.

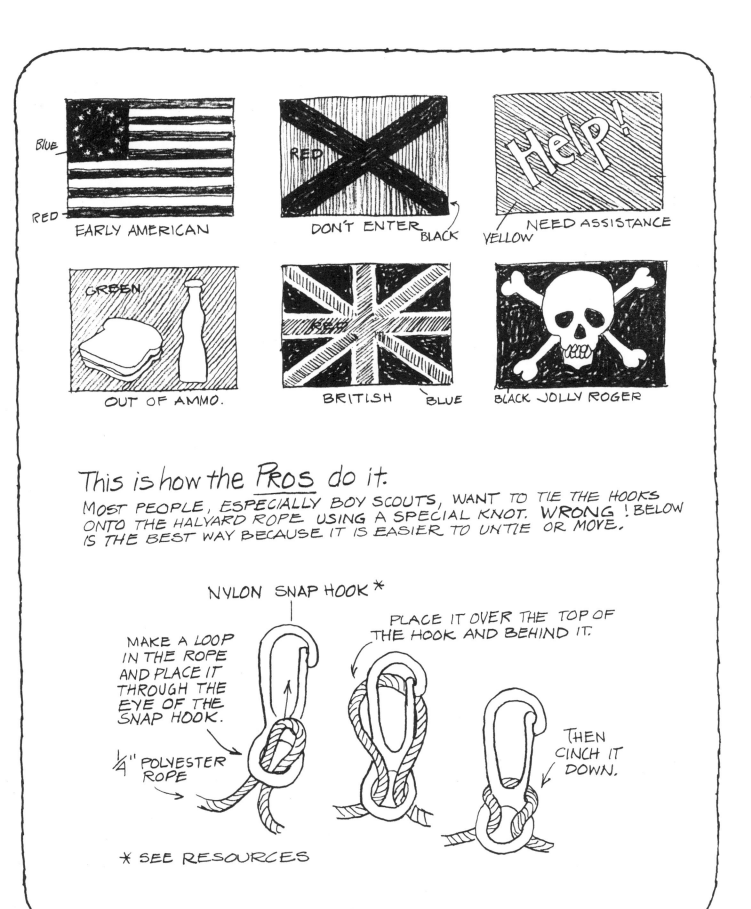

BLUE
RED
EARLY AMERICAN

RED
DON'T ENTER
BLACK

Help!
YELLOW
NEED ASSISTANCE

GREEN
OUT OF AMMO.

BRITISH
BLUE

BLACK JOLLY ROGER

This is how the Pros do it.

MOST PEOPLE, ESPECIALLY BOY SCOUTS, WANT TO TIE THE HOOKS ONTO THE HALYARD ROPE USING A SPECIAL KNOT. WRONG! BELOW IS THE BEST WAY BECAUSE IT IS EASIER TO UNTIE OR MOVE.

NYLON SNAP HOOK *

PLACE IT OVER THE TOP OF THE HOOK AND BEHIND IT.

MAKE A LOOP IN THE ROPE AND PLACE IT THROUGH THE EYE OF THE SNAP HOOK.

1/4" POLYESTER ROPE

THEN CINCH IT DOWN.

* SEE RESOURCES

How to Make a Five-Pointed Military Star

INSIGNIA

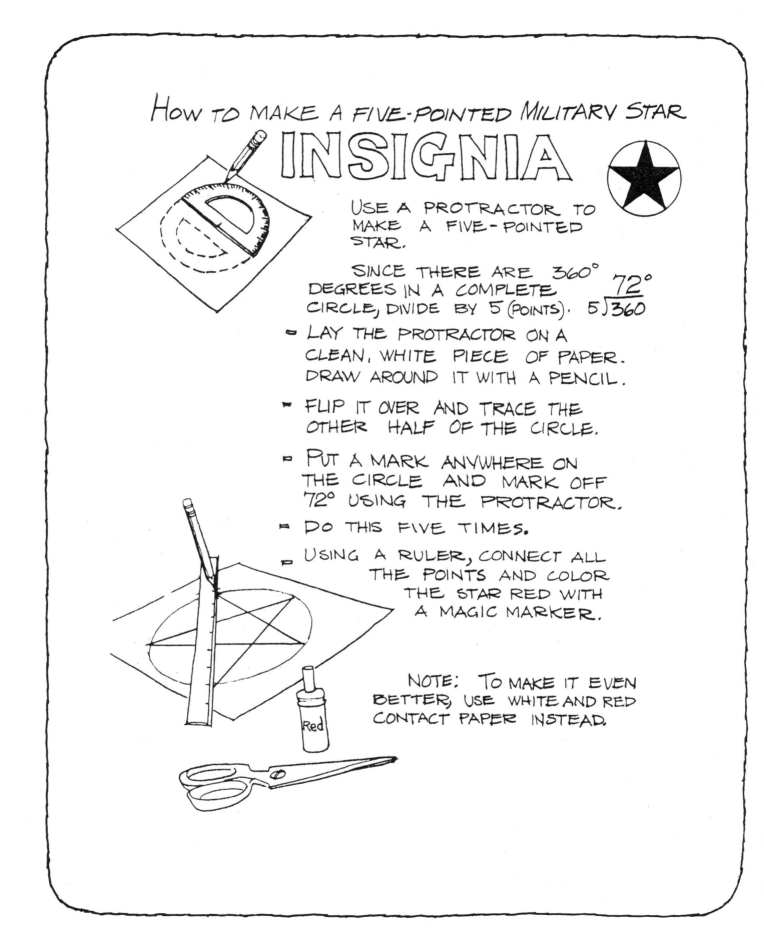

Use a protractor to make a five-pointed star.

Since there are 360° degrees in a complete circle, divide by 5 (points). $5\overline{)360}$ = 72°

- Lay the protractor on a clean, white piece of paper. Draw around it with a pencil.

- Flip it over and trace the other half of the circle.

- Put a mark anywhere on the circle and mark off 72° using the protractor.

- Do this five times.

- Using a ruler, connect all the points and color the star red with a magic marker.

Note: To make it even better, use white and red contact paper instead.

MODEL FORT

... MADE FROM PAPIER-MÂCHÉ OVER CHICKEN WIRE

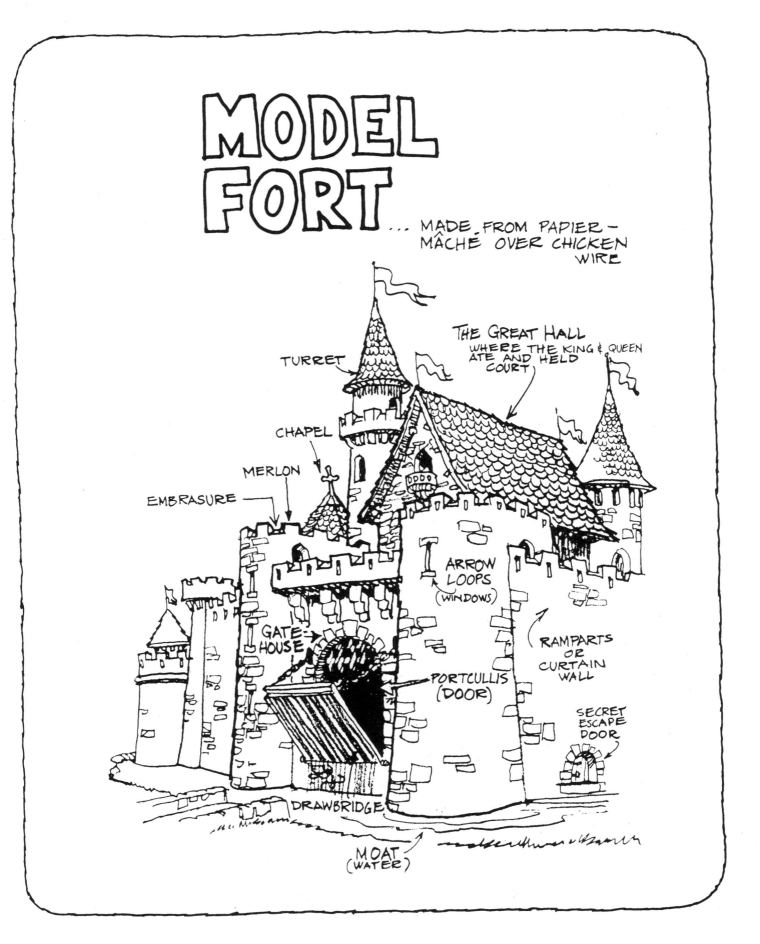

THE GREAT HALL
WHERE THE KING & QUEEN ATE AND HELD COURT

TURRET

CHAPEL

MERLON

EMBRASURE

ARROW LOOPS (WINDOWS)

GATE HOUSE

RAMPARTS OR CURTAIN WALL

PORTCULLIS (DOOR)

SECRET ESCAPE DOOR

DRAWBRIDGE

MOAT (WATER)

MODEL FORTS ARE FUN TO MAKE

AND FUN TO PLAY WITH WHEN THEY ARE FINISHED. YOU CAN BUY MINIATURE TOY KNIGHTS AND HORSES AND PUT THEM IN THE FORT. TOY STORES ALSO CARRY AN ARRAY OF SPECIAL SCALED-DOWN MEDIEVAL WAR TOYS LIKE CROSSBOWS, CATAPULTS, MORTARS, CANNONS, AND LADDERS FOR THE INVADING FORCES TO SCALE THE WALLS.

START WITH A 24"x 24" PIECE OF ½" PLYWOOD AS A BASE AND LAY OUT YOUR FORT WITH A PENCIL. MARK WHERE THE GATEHOUSE (ENTRANCE), GREAT HALL, STABLE, STOREHOUSE, CHAPEL, AND CORNER TOWERS SHOULD BE. A REAL FORT GENERALLY HAD AN OUTER AND AN INNER WALL OF DEFENSE. YOUR FORT CAN HAVE ONLY ONE WALL TO KEEP IT SIMPLE.

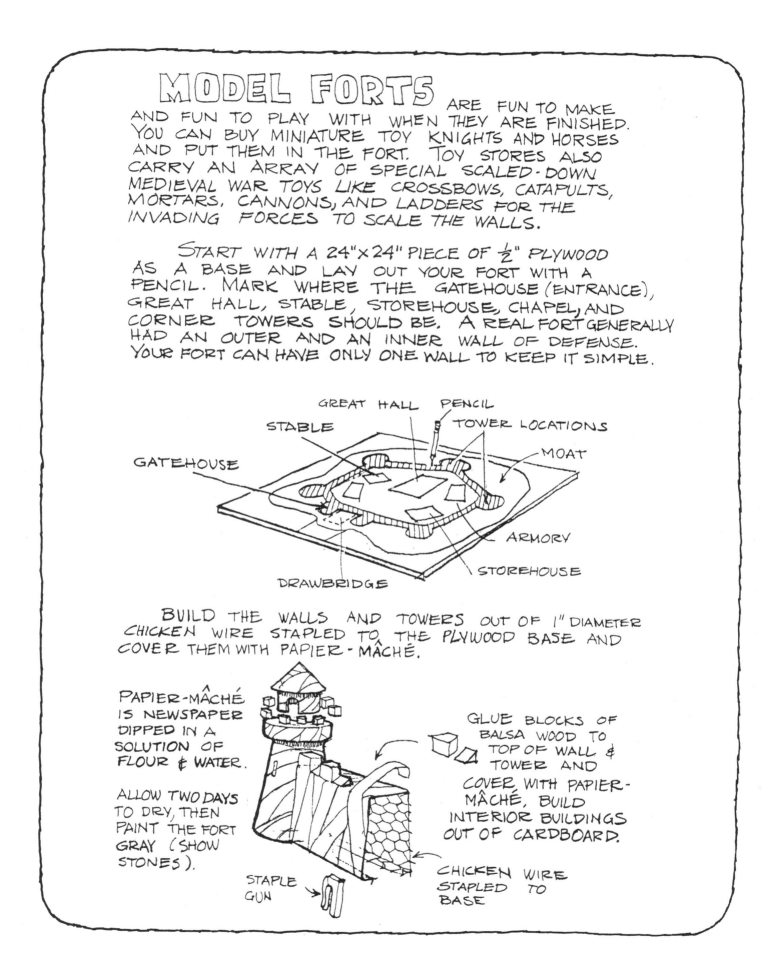

GREAT HALL   PENCIL

STABLE   TOWER LOCATIONS

GATEHOUSE   MOAT

ARMORY

STOREHOUSE

DRAWBRIDGE

BUILD THE WALLS AND TOWERS OUT OF 1" DIAMETER CHICKEN WIRE STAPLED TO THE PLYWOOD BASE AND COVER THEM WITH PAPIER-MÂCHÉ.

PAPIER-MÂCHÉ IS NEWSPAPER DIPPED IN A SOLUTION OF FLOUR & WATER.

ALLOW TWO DAYS TO DRY, THEN PAINT THE FORT GRAY (SHOW STONES).

STAPLE GUN

GLUE BLOCKS OF BALSA WOOD TO TOP OF WALL & TOWER AND COVER WITH PAPIER-MÂCHÉ, BUILD INTERIOR BUILDINGS OUT OF CARDBOARD.

CHICKEN WIRE STAPLED TO BASE

RESOURCES

Flag Hardware
The Flag Guys
(845) 562-0088
www.flagguys.com

Hand Tools
Harbor Freight Tools
(800) 444-3353
www.harborfreight.com

Hardware
Woodworker's Supply
(800) 645-9292
www.woodworker.com

Lumber and Hardware
Lowe's Companies, Inc.
(800) 445-6937
www.lowes.com

Power Tools
Hitachi Koki USA, Ltd.
(800) 706-7337
www.hitachipowertools.com

Rope (Hempex)
R&W Rope
(800)260-8599
www.rwrope.com

Wood Preservatives
Eco Wood Treatment
(250) 538-5516
www.ecowoodtreatment.com

LifeTime Wood Treatment
(250) 358-2661
www.valhalco.com

RECOMMENDED READING

Castle by David Macaulay

Catapult Design by Ron L. Toms

Books by David & Jeanie Stiles

Treehouses and Other Cool Stuff—50 Projects You Can Build

Treehouses, Huts & Forts

Fun Projects for You & the Kids

Treehouses You Can Actually Build

Treehouses & Playhouses You Can Build

Playhouses You Can Build

Cabins: A Guide to Building Your Own Retreat

Workshops You Can Build

Sheds: A Do-it-Yourself Guide, 3rd Edition

Rustic Retreats

Please visit our website at
www.stilesdesigns.com
and send us photographs
of your projects.
Thank you.

Stiles
Designs

stilesdesigns.com